Pranav Pandya is an accomplished IT professional with a remarkable career spanning four decades. With enriching experiences in India, the Middle East, the USA and Europe, he has established himself as a business development expert with a deep understanding of global markets. In recent years, he has embarked on a conscious journey to prioritise his other passions: photography, travelling, music, and writing. Born and raised in Mumbai, he draws inspiration from the city's vibrant culture, rich history and can-do attitude.

MIND-BODY MASTERY

Achieving Optimal Health & Productivity through Mindfulness & Meditation

PRANAV PANDYA

Inkfeathers Publishing
www.inkfeathers.com

AUTHOR'S NOTE

As we navigate the complexities of modern life, we often find ourselves searching for ways to improve our well-being and productivity. Many of us turn to various forms of self-help, from exercise routines to diets, in an effort to find the optimal path to success. Yet despite these efforts, we may still feel like something is missing.

That something, as many of us have discovered, is the mind-body connection. Our mind and body are not separate entities but rather deeply intertwined aspects of ourselves. In Mind-Body Mastery, I will take you, dear reader, on a journey to explore the fascinating connection between our mind and body and how we can harness this connection to achieve greater levels of health and productivity.

Through the power of mindfulness and meditation practices, Mind-Body Mastery offers a comprehensive guide to unlocking our full potential. The book is grounded in scientific research yet presented in a practical and accessible way that can be easily applied to our daily lives.

In these pages, you will learn how to cultivate a deeper sense of presence and calm, overcome mental obstacles, boost physical health, enhance productivity, develop positive habits, and strengthen the mind-body connection. The author provides a wealth of exercises and techniques, along with real-life examples and case studies, to help guide us on this journey.

Whether you're a seasoned practitioner or new to mindfulness and meditation practices, Mind-Body Mastery is an essential guide for anyone looking to achieve optimal health and productivity. I have no doubt that this book will serve as an invaluable resource for readers for years to come.

Pranav Pandya

CONTENTS

Chapter 1

THE MIND-BODY CONNECTION

The mind and body are not separate entities but rather deeply intertwined aspects of ourselves. This is the foundation of the mind-body connection, which has gained increasing attention in recent years for its role in our overall well-being and productivity. In this chapter, we will explore the fascinating connection between the mind and body and how it affects our health and productivity.

The History and Evolution of the Mind-Body Connection, From Ancient Eastern Practices to Modern Scientific Research

The history and evolution of the mind-body connection can be traced back to ancient Eastern practices, such as yoga and meditation. These practices emphasized the interconnectivity between the mind and body and sought to balance both aspects for optimal health and well-being. In traditional Chinese medicine, the concept of Qi (or life force energy) was used to explain the mind-body connection and how it influenced health.

In the Western world, the mind-body connection was often viewed with skepticism and dismissed as pseudoscience. However, the field of psychosomatic medicine emerged in the early 20th century, exploring the connection between psychological factors and physical health. Research in this area continued to grow throughout the 20th century, leading to the development of mind-body therapies such as biofeedback and relaxation techniques.

In the 1970s, the mind-body connection gained further attention with the emergence of the holistic health movement. This movement emphasized the importance of treating the whole person rather than just the physical symptoms of illness. It also brought attention to the impact of stress and negative emotions on health and well-being.

In recent years, modern scientific research has provided further evidence of the mind-body connection. Studies have shown that stress and negative emotions can have a significant impact on physical health, while mindfulness and meditation practices can improve immune function and reduce symptoms of depression and anxiety.

Today, the mind-body connection is widely recognized as an important aspect of overall health and well-being. It is a key component of many integrative and complementary medicine practices and is increasingly being integrated into mainstream medical care. By understanding the history and evolution of the mind-body connection, we can appreciate the importance of this concept and how it can help us achieve greater levels of health and productivity.

The Science Behind the Mind-Body Connection, Including the Role of the Nervous and Immune Systems in Regulating Our Physiological and Emotional Responses

The mind-body connection is a complex interplay between our thoughts, emotions, and physical health. In recent years, scientific research has begun to shed light on the underlying mechanisms of this connection. At the core of this research is the role of the nervous and immune systems in regulating our physiological and emotional responses.

The nervous system is responsible for controlling all bodily functions, from breathing and heart rate to digestion and movement. It is divided into two main branches: the sympathetic nervous system (SNS) and the parasympathetic nervous system (PNS). The SNS is activated in response to stress or danger, leading to the release of adrenaline and other stress hormones. This triggers the well-known "fight or flight" response, which prepares the body for action. The PNS, on the other hand, is responsible for promoting relaxation and restoring balance after a stressful event.

Research has shown that chronic stress and negative emotions can lead to dysregulation of the SNS and PNS, leading to a range of health problems, from cardiovascular disease to depression and anxiety. Mind-body practices, such as mindfulness and meditation, have been shown to activate the PNS and reduce the stress response, leading to improvements in overall health and well-being.

The immune system, meanwhile, is responsible for protecting the body against infection and disease. It is a complex network of cells, tissues, and organs that work together to recognize and destroy harmful invaders. Research has shown that the immune system is also influenced by our emotions and thoughts. Negative emotions, such as stress and anxiety, can lead to immune dysfunction, while positive emotions, such as happiness and gratitude, can boost immune function.

One key player in the mind-body-immune connection is the hypothalamic-pituitary-adrenal (HPA) axis. This system involves the release of stress hormones, such as cortisol, in response to stress or negative emotions. Chronic activation of the HPA axis can lead to immune dysfunction and increased susceptibility to illness.

By understanding the role of the nervous and immune systems in the mind-body connection, we can begin to appreciate the importance of practices that promote relaxation, mindfulness, and emotional regulation.

The Impact of Stress and Negative Emotions on our Health and Productivity and How the Mind-Body Connection can be Harnessed to Counteract these Effects

Stress and negative emotions can have a profound impact on our health and productivity. Chronic stress has been linked to a range of health problems, from cardiovascular disease to mental health disorders. Negative emotions, such as anxiety and depression, can also impair cognitive function and decrease productivity.

Fortunately, the mind-body connection offers a powerful tool for counteracting the negative effects of stress and negative emotions. Practices such as mindfulness, meditation, and yoga have been shown to reduce stress and anxiety, improve mood, and increase productivity.

Research has shown that mindfulness, in particular, can have a positive impact on our health and well-being. Mindfulness involves paying attention to the present moment without judgment or distraction. By bringing our attention to the present, we can reduce the tendency to ruminate on past regrets or worry about future events, which can fuel stress and anxiety.

In addition to reducing stress and negative emotions, mindfulness has also been shown to have a positive impact on our physical health. Studies have found that mindfulness can reduce blood pressure, improve sleep, and boost immune function.

Meditation is another powerful tool for harnessing the mind-body connection. Like mindfulness, meditation involves bringing our attention to the present moment, but it also involves a more structured practice of focused attention or visualization. Studies have found that regular meditation practice can lead to changes in brain structure and function, including increased gray matter density in areas associated with attention and emotional regulation.

Yoga is yet another practice that can promote the mind-body connection and improve health and productivity. Yoga involves a series of poses and movements, often combined with breathwork and meditation. Research has shown that yoga can reduce stress and anxiety, improve sleep quality, and boost immune function.

By incorporating mindfulness, meditation, or yoga into their daily routines, readers can begin to harness the power of the mind-body connection to counteract the negative effects of stress and negative emotions.

The Benefits of Cultivating a Strong Mind-Body Connection Include Reduced Stress and Anxiety, Improved Immune Function, Better Sleep, and Enhanced Cognitive Function

Cultivating a strong mind-body connection can have a wide range of benefits for our health and well-being. By harnessing the power of our thoughts and emotions to influence our physical state, we can improve our overall health and productivity.

One of the most well-known benefits of the mind-body connection is its ability to reduce stress and anxiety. Chronic stress can take a toll on our physical and mental health, leading to a range of health problems, including cardiovascular disease, depression, and anxiety disorders. By practicing mindfulness, meditation, or yoga, we can learn to manage our stress levels more effectively and improve our overall quality of life.

Research has also shown that a strong mind-body connection can have a positive impact on immune function. When we experience stress or negative emotions, our bodies release hormones such as cortisol and adrenaline, which can suppress the immune system. By practicing relaxation techniques, such as mindfulness or yoga, we can counteract this effect and boost our immune function.

Another benefit of the mind-body connection is better sleep quality. Sleep is critical for our overall health and well-being, and chronic sleep deprivation has been linked to a range of health problems, including obesity, diabetes, and cardiovascular disease. By practicing relaxation techniques before bed, such as meditation or deep breathing, we can improve the quality of our sleep and wake up feeling more refreshed and alert.

Finally, a strong mind-body connection can enhance cognitive function, including memory, attention, and decision-making. By reducing stress and anxiety, we can improve our ability to focus and concentrate, and by practicing mindfulness or meditation, we can enhance our cognitive flexibility and creativity.

Cultivating a strong mind-body connection can have a wide range of benefits for our health and productivity. By reducing stress and anxiety, improving immune function, enhancing sleep quality, and boosting cognitive function, we can optimize our physical and mental well-being and achieve greater success in all areas of our lives. In the following section of this chapter, we will explore practical exercises and techniques for cultivating a strong mind-body connection and reaping these benefits for ourselves.

Practical Exercises and Techniques

- **Body Scan Meditation:** This exercise involves scanning your body from head to toe, paying attention to any physical sensations or areas of tension. By practicing this exercise regularly, you can become more attuned to your body's signals and better equipped to respond to stress or discomfort.

- **Deep Breathing:** Take a few deep breaths, inhaling through your nose and exhaling through your mouth. As you inhale, imagine filling your lungs with fresh, clean air. As you exhale, imagine releasing any tension or negativity from your body.

- **Mindful Movement**: Engage in a physical activity that requires focus and concentration, such as yoga or tai chi. By practicing mindful movement, you can strengthen the mind-body connection and cultivate a sense of inner calm and balance.

- **Gratitude Practice:** Take a few moments each day to reflect on what you are grateful for. This can help shift your focus away from negative emotions and toward positive experiences, strengthening the mind-body connection and promoting overall well-being.

By incorporating these exercises and techniques into your daily life, you can cultivate a stronger mind-body connection and achieve greater levels of well-being and productivity.

Chapter 2

MINDFULNESS: THE POWER OF PRESENCE

Mindfulness is the practice of being fully present and engaged in the present moment without judgment or distraction. It has become an increasingly popular technique for reducing stress and anxiety, enhancing focus and productivity, and improving overall well-being.

In this chapter, we will explore the power of mindfulness and how it can help us achieve optimal health and productivity. We will begin by discussing the basic principles of mindfulness and the benefits of incorporating it into our daily lives.

The Basic Principles of Mindfulness and the Benefits of Incorporating it into Our Daily Lives

At its core, mindfulness is the practice of being fully present and engaged in the present moment. It involves paying attention to our thoughts, emotions, and physical sensations without judgment or distraction. By doing so, we can cultivate a greater sense of awareness and clarity, reduce stress and anxiety, and enhance our overall well-being.

One of the key principles of mindfulness is non-judgmental awareness. This means learning to observe our thoughts, emotions, and physical sensations without judging them as good or bad, right or wrong. By doing so, we can cultivate greater self-awareness and compassion and reduce the negative impact of self-criticism or self-doubt.

Another key principle of mindfulness is acceptance. This involves accepting things as they are in the present moment rather than trying to change or control them. By accepting our experiences, we can reduce resistance and anxiety and cultivate greater peace and contentment.

Incorporating mindfulness into our daily lives can have many benefits. One of the most significant benefits is its ability to reduce stress and anxiety.

By learning to be fully present and engaged in the present moment, we can reduce the negative impact of stress on our physical and mental health and improve our overall quality of life.

Mindfulness can also enhance our focus and productivity. By learning to be fully present in our work, we can improve our ability to concentrate and make better decisions. We can also reduce distractions and improve our ability to manage our time effectively.

In addition to these benefits, mindfulness can also improve our relationships with others. By being fully present and engaged in our interactions with others, we can improve our communication skills and deepen our connections with those around us. We can also reduce conflicts and misunderstandings and cultivate greater empathy and compassion.

To incorporate mindfulness into our daily lives, we can practice mindfulness meditation, deep breathing exercises, or mindful movement practices such as yoga or tai chi. By dedicating a few minutes each day to these practices, we can experience the many benefits of mindfulness and achieve optimal health and productivity.

One of the key benefits of mindfulness is its ability to reduce stress and anxiety. When we practice mindfulness, we learn to focus our attention on the present moment rather than getting caught up in worries or fears about the future or regrets about the past. By doing so, we can reduce the negative impact of stress on our physical and mental health and improve our overall quality of life.

Mindfulness and its Ability to Reduce Stress and Anxiety

Mindfulness is the practice of being fully present and engaged in the current moment without judgment or distraction. By cultivating mindfulness, we can develop the ability to observe our thoughts and emotions without becoming attached to them, which can help us better manage stress and anxiety.

Studies have shown that mindfulness-based interventions can significantly reduce symptoms of stress and anxiety in individuals, including those with clinical anxiety disorders. This is because mindfulness can help regulate our physiological responses to stress, including our heart rate and cortisol levels. When we practice mindfulness, we are better able to respond to stress in a more calm and controlled manner rather than reacting impulsively or becoming overwhelmed.

Incorporating mindfulness practices into our daily routines can be as simple as taking a few minutes each day to focus on our breath, observe our surroundings, or engage in mindful movements such as yoga or tai chi. Through consistent practice, we can cultivate a greater sense of calm and well-being, which can have a positive impact on our overall health and productivity.

In this chapter, we will explore various mindfulness techniques and exercises that readers can incorporate into their daily lives to reduce stress and anxiety. We will also examine the scientific research behind mindfulness and its effectiveness in promoting mental and physical health. By the end of this chapter, readers will have a better understanding of the power of mindfulness and how to begin integrating it into their daily routines.

In addition to reducing stress and anxiety, mindfulness can also enhance our focus and productivity. By learning to be fully present and engaged in our work, we can improve our ability to concentrate and make better decisions. We can also reduce distractions and improve our ability to manage our time effectively.

Mindfulness and its Ability to Enhance Our Focus and Productivity

Mindfulness practices, such as meditation and breath awareness, can help us train our minds to stay present and focused on the task at hand. By developing the ability to stay present and avoid distractions, we can improve our productivity and achieve more in less time.

Studies have shown that mindfulness-based interventions can improve cognitive function, including attention and working memory. This is because mindfulness can help us better regulate our thoughts and emotions, which can prevent us from becoming distracted by worries or external stimuli. By practicing mindfulness, we can train our brains to remain focused on the present moment, which can enhance our ability to complete tasks and achieve our goals.

Incorporating mindfulness practices into our daily routines can be as simple as taking a few minutes each day to focus on our breath or engage in mindful movement. By consistently practicing mindfulness, we can develop a greater ability to concentrate and stay focused, which can improve our productivity and overall well-being.

Another benefit of mindfulness is its ability to improve our relationships with others. By being fully present and engaged in our interactions with others, we can improve our communication skills and deepen our connections with those around us. We can also reduce conflicts and misunderstandings and cultivate greater empathy and compassion.

Mindfulness and its Ability to Improve Our Relationships with Others

Mindfulness practices can help us become more aware of our thoughts, emotions, and behaviors, which can help us relate to others with greater empathy and understanding.

When we practice mindfulness, we learn to become more aware of our own reactions and patterns of behavior. This can help us recognize when we are reacting out of habit rather than responding with intention. By becoming more aware of our own emotions and behaviors, we can become more understanding of others and better able to relate to their experiences.

In addition to improving our self-awareness, mindfulness can also help us become better listeners and communicators. When we are fully present at the moment, we are better able to listen to others without judgment or distraction. By practicing active listening and empathy, we can improve our ability to connect with others and build stronger relationships.

Research has shown that mindfulness-based interventions can improve relationship satisfaction and reduce conflict in romantic relationships. Mindfulness can also help us become more compassionate and accepting of others, which can improve our relationships with family members, friends, and coworkers.

Practical exercises and techniques for cultivating mindfulness include mindfulness meditation, deep breathing exercises, and mindful movement practices such as yoga or tai chi. By incorporating these practices into our daily lives, we can experience the many benefits of mindfulness and achieve optimal health and productivity.

In the following sections of this chapter, we will explore these practices in greater detail and provide practical tips for incorporating mindfulness into our daily routines. With practice and dedication, we can cultivate the power of presence and achieve greater success and fulfillment in all areas of our lives.

Mindfulness is about being fully present at the moment, without judgment or distraction. It is about paying attention to what is happening right now rather than dwelling on the past or worrying about the future.

By developing a mindful awareness of our thoughts, feelings, and sensations, we can learn to better regulate our emotions and reduce stress and anxiety. Mindfulness has been shown to be effective in a wide range of settings, from the workplace to the classroom, and can help us become more focused and productive in our daily lives.

In addition to traditional mindfulness practices such as seated meditation, there are many other practices that can help us cultivate the power of presence and achieve optimal health and productivity. Yoga and tai chi, for example, are ancient practices that combine physical movement with breath awareness and mindfulness.

Yoga is a practice that originated in ancient India and has gained popularity in recent years for its numerous health benefits, including improved flexibility, strength, and balance. Yoga was developed as a way to achieve spiritual enlightenment and unity with the divine. Over time, yoga evolved to include physical postures (*asanas*) and breathing exercises (*pranayama*) that promote physical health and well-being.

Beyond the physical benefits, yoga also incorporates breath awareness and meditation to help practitioners cultivate mindfulness and reduce stress and anxiety. There are many different styles of yoga, so it is important to find one that resonates with you and fits your individual needs and preferences.

Tai chi, on the other hand, is a Chinese martial art that emphasizes slow, flowing movements and deep breathing. Like yoga, tai chi has been shown to have numerous health benefits, including improved balance, flexibility, and cognitive function. Tai chi also incorporates mindfulness and meditation, with practitioners focusing on the present moment and connecting with their breath and body.

The basic principles of yoga and tai chi both involve the integration of body, breath and mind to promote overall health and well-being. Both practices emphasize the importance of mindfulness and present-moment awareness, with a focus on being fully present in each moment and cultivating a sense of inner peace and calm.

Incorporating mindfulness into our daily routines can be done through formal meditation or simple mindfulness exercises that can be practiced throughout the day. Formal meditation can involve sitting quietly and focusing on the breath or a specific object, while mindfulness exercises can be as simple as taking a few deep breaths before a stressful meeting or focusing on the sensations of the body while washing dishes.

Practical tips for incorporating mindfulness into daily routines can include setting aside a specific time each day for formal meditation, taking breaks throughout the day to focus on the breath and tune into the body, and incorporating mindful movement practices such as yoga or tai chi into a regular exercise routine. By exploring these practices in greater detail and incorporating mindfulness into daily routines, we can experience the many benefits of mindfulness and achieve optimal health and productivity in all areas of our lives.

While details of practices in Yoga or Tai chi are beyond the scope of this book, I would encourage you to seek professional guidance from a Master of Yoga or Tai chi to explore which exercises work best for you. This should be done in consultation with your doctor to make sure that you ease into regular practice without causing any short or long-term harm to your body.

Chapter 3

MEDITATION: THE ART OF INNER STILLNESS

Meditation is a powerful tool that allows us to cultivate inner stillness and develop a greater sense of self-awareness. It is a practice that has been used for centuries by individuals from all walks of life to enhance their mental, emotional, and physical well-being. In this chapter, we will explore the art of meditation and its ability to help us achieve a greater sense of inner peace and clarity.

We will start by delving into the history and evolution of meditation, tracing its roots back to ancient Eastern practices such as Hinduism and Buddhism. We will discuss the various forms of meditation, including mindfulness meditation, loving-kindness meditation, and transcendental meditation, and explore their unique benefits and techniques.

Meditation

Meditation is an ancient practice that has been around for thousands of years, with roots in Eastern spiritual traditions such as Hinduism and Buddhism. The earliest recorded evidence of meditation dates back to approximately 500 BCE in India, where it was originally used as a tool for spiritual enlightenment and self-discovery.

Over time, meditation practices evolved and spread throughout

Asia, eventually making their way to the West in the 20th century. Today, meditation is a widely practiced and well-researched method for reducing stress and improving overall well-being.

There are many different types of meditation, each with its own unique techniques and benefits. One of the most widely practiced forms of meditation is mindfulness meditation, which involves focusing on the present moment and cultivating a non-judgmental awareness of one's thoughts, feelings, and sensations.

Loving-kindness meditation, on the other hand, involves focusing on feelings of love, kindness, and compassion toward oneself and others. This type of meditation has been shown to improve empathy, social connectedness, and emotional well-being.

Transcendental meditation, or TM, is a form of meditation that involves the use of a mantra, or repeated sound or phrase, to help calm the mind and achieve a state of deep relaxation. TM has been shown to reduce stress and anxiety, as well as improve cognitive function and overall well-being.

Additionally, we will provide practical tips for incorporating meditation into our daily routines, including advice on finding the right type of meditation for our individual needs and preferences, as well as strategies for overcoming common obstacles to regular practice. By cultivating the art of inner stillness through meditation, we can achieve greater clarity, focus, and inner peace in all aspects of our lives.

We will also examine the science behind meditation, including its effects on the brain and body. Studies have shown that regular meditation can help reduce stress and anxiety, improve cognitive function, and even boost the immune system. Through the practice of meditation, we can learn to manage our thoughts and emotions more effectively, leading to greater clarity and focus in all areas of our lives.

Incorporating meditation into our daily routine can be a powerful tool for achieving inner stillness, reducing stress, and improving overall well-being.

Here are some practical tips for incorporating meditation into our daily routines:

1. **Start with short sessions:** If you're new to meditation, start with short sessions of 5-10 minutes and gradually increase the duration as you become more comfortable.

2. **Choose a quiet and comfortable space**: Find a quiet space where you won't be disturbed, and sit on a comfortable cushion or chair with your back straight and your feet firmly planted on the ground.

3. **Focus on your breath:** Focus your attention on your breath, taking deep, slow breaths in and out through your nose.

4. **Be patient and non-judgmental:** Be patient with yourself, and don't judge yourself if your mind wanders. Simply bring your attention back to your breath each time you become aware of your thoughts.

5. **Experiment with different types of meditation:** There are many different types of meditation, such as mindfulness meditation, loving-kindness meditation, and transcendental meditation. Experiment with different types to find the one that resonates with you.

6. **Use guided meditations:** Guided meditations can be a helpful tool for beginners, as they provide instruction and guidance throughout the meditation session.

7. **Make it a daily habit:** Consistency is key when it comes to meditation. Try to set aside time each day for your meditation practice, even if it's just a few minutes.

Remember, there is no one-size-fits-all approach to meditation. It's important to find the type of meditation that works best for you and your individual needs and preferences. With practice and dedication, incorporating meditation into your daily routine can help you achieve greater inner stillness and improve your overall well-being.

Examining the Science Behind Meditation, including its Effects on the Brain and Body

Meditation has been shown to have a profound impact on the brain and body. Studies have found that regular meditation practice can increase the density of gray matter in the brain, particularly in areas associated with learning, memory, and emotional regulation. Meditation has also been found to reduce activity in the amygdala, the brain's fear center, and increase activity in the prefrontal cortex, which is involved in executive functions such as decision-making and impulse control.

Additionally, research has shown that meditation can have positive effects on the body, including reducing inflammation, lowering blood pressure, and improving immune function. These effects are believed to be related to the reduction in stress that meditation can provide. By lowering the body's stress response, meditation can help to reduce the negative effects of chronic stress on the body.

One study found that meditation can even have a positive impact on the expression of genes related to inflammation and immune function. The study found that after just eight weeks of meditation practice, participants had changes in the expression of genes related to inflammation and the body's response to stress.

As discussed above, there have been many studies conducted on the effects of meditation on the brain and body. Here are some examples:

1. A study published in the journal NeuroImage found that eight weeks of mindfulness meditation training led to changes in the brain's default mode network, a network of brain regions associated with self-referential thinking and mind wandering. Participants who underwent mindfulness meditation training showed reduced activity in this network during a task that required attention, suggesting that they were better able to focus their attention and regulate their thoughts.

2. Another study published in the journal Frontiers in Human Neuroscience found that participants who underwent an eight-week mindfulness meditation program showed improvements in their ability to regulate their emotions, as well as changes in brain activity in regions associated with emotion regulation.

3. A study published in the journal Brain, Behavior, and Immunity found that participants who underwent a three-month meditation and yoga program had lower levels of inflammatory markers in their blood compared to a control group. Inflammation has been linked to a variety of health problems, including cardiovascular disease, diabetes, and depression.

4. A study published in the journal PLOS ONE found that participants who underwent a mindfulness meditation program had improvements in their working memory capacity, as well as changes in brain activity in regions associated with working memory.

These are just a few examples of the many studies that have been conducted on the effects of meditation. Research suggests that meditation can have a variety of positive effects on both the brain and body, including improvements in attention, emotion regulation, working memory, and immune function. We can summarize that Meditation can have a profound impact on both the brain and body, leading to improved health and well-being.

Chapter 4

OVERCOMING MENTAL OBSTACLES

In this chapter, we will explore the common mental obstacles that can hinder our progress toward optimal health and productivity and provide practical strategies for overcoming them. These obstacles can take many forms, such as negative self-talk, limiting beliefs, fear, self-doubt, and procrastination.

Negative self-talk is a common obstacle that can lead to feelings of inadequacy, low self-esteem, and a lack of motivation. It can be difficult to break free from negative self-talk, but it is possible with practice and dedication. One way to overcome negative self-talk is to reframe our thoughts and focus on positive affirmations. We can also practice mindfulness to become more aware of our thoughts and learn to let go of negative self-talk.

Exploring One of the Most Common Mental Obstacles: Negative Self-Talk

Let us will explore one of the most common mental obstacles that many of us face: negative self-talk. Negative self-talk refers to the inner monologue that we have with ourselves, often criticizing and belittling our abilities, achievements, and self-worth.

Negative self-talk can take many forms, such as self-doubt, self-blame, and self-criticism. It can be triggered by various situations, such as failure, rejection, or criticism from others. Negative self-talk can have a profound impact on our mental health, leading to anxiety, depression, and low self-esteem.

Fortunately, there are many ways to overcome negative self-talk. One powerful technique is mindfulness. Mindfulness simply means maintaining a moment-by-moment awareness of our thoughts, feelings, bodily sensations, and the surrounding environment through a gentle, nurturing, and non-judgmental lens.

By practicing mindfulness, we can learn to observe our negative thoughts without becoming attached to them, allowing them to pass by like clouds in the sky.

Another technique is cognitive-behavioral therapy (CBT), which involves identifying and challenging negative thoughts and beliefs. CBT can help us reframe our negative self-talk into more positive and realistic statements, improving our overall mental health and well-being.

Additionally, positive affirmations, visualization, and self-compassion can also be effective tools for overcoming negative self-talk. By consciously choosing to focus on our strengths and accomplishments, visualizing positive outcomes, and treating ourselves with kindness and compassion, we can cultivate a more positive and supportive inner dialogue.

Overall, overcoming negative self-talk is an important step toward achieving optimal mental health and productivity. By practicing mindfulness, cognitive-behavioral therapy, positive affirmations, visualization, and self-compassion, we can develop a more positive and empowering relationship with ourselves, allowing us to overcome obstacles and achieve our goals with greater ease and confidence.

Limiting Beliefs Can Also Hold Us Back from Reaching Our Full Potential.

These beliefs are often based on past experiences or societal expectations and can limit our ability to take risks and try new things. To overcome limiting beliefs, we must first identify them and challenge their validity. We can do this by asking ourselves questions such as "Where did this belief come from?" and "Is this belief serving me or holding me back?" By questioning our limiting beliefs, we can begin to replace them with more empowering ones.

Limiting beliefs are basically deeply ingrained thoughts or ideas that we hold about ourselves, others, or the world around us that hold us back from reaching our full potential. These beliefs can be formed early in life through experiences or external influences and can become so deeply ingrained that we may not even be aware of their existence.

Examples of limiting beliefs include thoughts such as "I'm not good enough," "I don't have what it takes," or "I'll never be successful." These beliefs can cause feelings of self-doubt, anxiety, and fear and can ultimately prevent us from taking the necessary steps to achieve our goals.

Overcoming limiting beliefs requires a deep understanding of ourselves and our thought patterns. We must become aware of these beliefs and challenge them, replacing them with positive affirmations and self-talk. This can be achieved through practices such as cognitive behavioral therapy, positive visualization, and mindfulness meditation.

One effective technique for challenging limiting beliefs is to ask ourselves questions such as, "Is this belief really true?" or "What evidence do I have to support this belief?" By questioning our beliefs, we can begin to break down the barriers that they create and open ourselves up to new possibilities.

Another powerful tool for overcoming limiting beliefs is to surround ourselves with positive influences, such as supportive friends and mentors who can provide encouragement and guidance. By building a network of positive relationships, we can strengthen our own sense of self-worth and cultivate the confidence needed to overcome our limiting beliefs.

Ultimately, overcoming limiting beliefs requires a commitment to personal growth and a willingness to step outside of our comfort zones. With dedication and perseverance, we can break free from the constraints of our limiting beliefs and achieve our full potential.

Fear is another common obstacle that can prevent us from taking action and pursuing our goals. Whether it is fear of failure, fear of the unknown, or fear of rejection, it can be paralyzing. To overcome fear, we must first acknowledge it and understand its underlying cause. We can then take small steps towards facing our fears and building confidence. It can also be helpful to practice visualization and positive self-talk to prepare for challenging situations.

Overcoming Fear

Fear is a natural human emotion that is designed to protect us from danger. However, when fear becomes excessive or irrational, it can hold us back from reaching our full potential and living a fulfilling life. Fear can manifest itself in many ways, such as fear of failure, fear of rejection, fear of the unknown, and even fear of success. If left unchecked, fear can lead to anxiety, stress, and even depression.

Fortunately, there are effective strategies for overcoming fear and cultivating a sense of courage and resilience. Mindfulness meditation, for example, can help us develop a more balanced and compassionate relationship with our emotions, including fear. By cultivating a non-judgmental awareness of our thoughts and feelings, we can learn to observe our fears without being overwhelmed by them.

Another powerful tool for overcoming fear is cognitive-behavioral therapy (CBT). CBT helps us identify and challenge our negative thought patterns and beliefs that contribute to our fears. By reframing our thoughts and beliefs in a more positive and realistic light, we can reduce the intensity and frequency of our fears.

Additionally, exposure therapy can help us confront our fears in a safe and controlled manner. By gradually exposing ourselves to the things we fear, we can desensitize ourselves to them and learn to tolerate them without experiencing overwhelming anxiety.

Other helpful strategies for overcoming fear include physical exercise, deep breathing techniques, and visualization exercises. By incorporating these practices into our daily routines, we can strengthen our emotional resilience and develop a sense of courage and confidence.

It's important to remember that overcoming fear is not a one-time event but rather an ongoing process. It requires patience, persistence, and a willingness to step outside our comfort zone. With time and practice, we can learn to overcome our fears and live a more fulfilling and courageous life.

Self-doubt can also be a major obstacle that prevents us from taking action and achieving our goals. It can be difficult to believe in ourselves, especially when faced with setbacks or challenges. To overcome self-doubt, we must first recognize it as a normal part of the human experience. We can then practice self-compassion and focus on our strengths and past successes. It can also be helpful to seek support from others and surround ourselves with positive influences.

Defeating Self Doubt

Defeating self-doubt is an essential step toward achieving optimal health and productivity. Self-doubt is the inner critic that constantly questions our abilities and undermines our confidence. It can manifest in various ways, including imposter syndrome, fear of failure, and perfectionism.

One way to defeat self-doubt is to challenge our negative self-talk. When we catch ourselves thinking negative thoughts such as "I'm not good enough" or "I can't do this," we can ask ourselves if there is any evidence to support these beliefs. Often, we will find that our self-doubt is based on unfounded assumptions or distorted thinking patterns.

Another way to overcome self-doubt is to set realistic goals and break them down into manageable steps. By achieving small victories along the way, we build confidence and momentum toward larger goals.

Meditation and mindfulness practices can also help us overcome self-doubt. By cultivating a non-judgmental awareness of our thoughts and emotions, we can observe our self-doubt without getting caught up in it. This can help us develop a more balanced perspective and reduce the power of our inner critic.

Finally, seeking support from others can also be helpful in overcoming self-doubt. Talking to a trusted friend, mentor, or therapist can provide us with validation, encouragement, and new perspectives on our abilities and strengths.

Procrastination is another obstacle that can hinder our progress toward optimal health and productivity. It can be tempting to put off tasks or avoid them altogether, but this only leads to more stress and anxiety. To overcome procrastination, we must first identify the root cause of our procrastination, whether it is fear, lack of motivation, or overwhelm. We can then break tasks down into smaller, manageable steps and set realistic deadlines. It can also be helpful to eliminate distractions and create a supportive environment for productivity.

Clearing the Obstacle of Procrastination

Procrastination can be a major obstacle to achieving our goals and fulfilling our potential. It can keep us from taking action on important tasks and lead to feelings of guilt, anxiety, and stress. However, by understanding the reasons behind our procrastination and implementing specific strategies, we can overcome this mental obstacle and become more productive and successful.

One of the key reasons for procrastination is a fear of failure or a lack of confidence in our ability to succeed. We may worry that if we start a task, we will not be able to complete it to our satisfaction or that we will face criticism or rejection from others. To overcome this obstacle it is important to shift our mindset from one of self-doubt to one of self-confidence. This can be achieved through positive self-talk, visualization, and setting achievable goals.

Another reason for procrastination is a lack of clarity or direction. We may feel overwhelmed by the complexity of a task or unsure of where to start. In this case, it can be helpful to break the task down into smaller, more manageable steps and create a clear plan of action. Setting specific deadlines and holding ourselves accountable can also help to keep us on track.

Distractions can also be a major obstacle to productivity and lead to procrastination. In today's digital age, we are constantly bombarded with notifications and information, making it easy to get sidetracked from our goals. To overcome this obstacle, it is important to create a distraction-free environment and set clear boundaries with technology. This can involve turning off notifications, limiting social media use, and taking regular breaks to refresh our minds.

Finally, procrastination can be caused by a lack of motivation or passion for the task at hand. In this case, it can be helpful to find ways to connect with our purpose and identify the deeper meaning behind the task. This can involve setting meaningful goals, focusing on the positive impact of our actions, and finding inspiration from others who have overcome similar challenges.

By understanding the reasons behind our procrastination and implementing specific strategies to overcome this mental obstacle, we can become more productive, fulfilled, and successful in all areas of our lives.

As we conclude this chapter, we can see overcoming mental obstacles is a key component of achieving optimal health and productivity. By recognizing and addressing negative self-talk, limiting beliefs, fear, self-doubt, and procrastination, we can break free from these obstacles and reach our full potential. With practice and dedication, we can cultivate a mindset of growth and resilience and achieve greater success and fulfillment in all areas of our lives.

Chapter 5

BOOSTING PHYSICAL HEALTH

Physical health is an essential aspect of overall wellness. It affects our ability to function optimally, both mentally and physically. In this chapter, we will explore various ways to boost physical health, including exercise, nutrition, sleep, and stress management.

Exercise

Regular exercise is essential for maintaining good physical health. Physical activity not only helps to build stronger muscles and bones, but it also improves cardiovascular health, reduces the risk of chronic diseases, helps with weight management, and boosts mood and overall wellbeing. In this chapter, we will discuss the importance of exercise for optimal health and productivity, the various types of exercise, and practical tips for incorporating exercise into our daily routines.

Importance of Exercise for Optimal Health and Productivity: Regular exercise has a host of benefits for both physical and mental health. It is essential for maintaining a healthy weight, reducing the risk of chronic diseases such as heart disease, stroke, and diabetes, improving cardiovascular health, and boosting overall physical fitness. Exercise also plays a critical role in mental health, helping to reduce stress, anxiety, and depression and improving mood and overall well-being. In addition to the physical and mental health benefits, regular exercise can also improve cognitive function and productivity, helping to enhance focus, creativity, and mental clarity.

Types of Exercise: There are many different types of exercise, each with its own unique benefits. Some of the most popular types of exercise include:

1. Aerobic Exercise

Aerobic exercise is a type of physical activity that involves the use of large muscle groups to increase the body's demand for oxygen. This increased demand leads to improved cardiovascular and respiratory function, as well as a host of other health benefits. Examples of aerobic exercise include running, swimming, cycling, and brisk walking.

One of the key benefits of aerobic exercise is improved cardiovascular health. Regular aerobic exercise can lower blood pressure, improve cholesterol levels, and reduce the risk of heart disease and stroke. It also strengthens the heart and lungs, making them more efficient at delivering oxygen and nutrients to the body's tissues.

Aerobic exercise also has benefits for weight management. It can help to burn calories and improve metabolism, making it easier to maintain a healthy weight. It also has positive effects on blood sugar levels, which can help to reduce the risk of type 2 diabetes.

In addition to these physical benefits, aerobic exercise is also good for mental health. It can help to reduce stress and anxiety, improve mood, and promote better sleep. It may also have cognitive benefits, such as improving memory and cognitive function.

To incorporate aerobic exercise into your routine, it is recommended to aim for at least 150 minutes of moderate-intensity aerobic exercise or 75 minutes of vigorous-intensity aerobic exercise per week, spread out over at least three days per week. It is important to start slowly and gradually increase the intensity and duration of exercise over time to avoid injury and ensure a sustainable habit. It is also important to choose activities that you enjoy, and that fit your lifestyle, such as going for a daily walk or joining a group fitness class.

2. Strength Training

Strength training, also known as resistance training, is a form of physical exercise that involves the use of weights, resistance bands, or other equipment to strengthen and tone muscles. Unlike aerobic exercise, which focuses on cardiovascular health and endurance, strength training is primarily aimed at building muscle mass, improving bone density, and increasing overall strength.

There are many different types of strength training exercises, ranging from traditional weightlifting exercises, such as bench presses and squats, to bodyweight exercises, such as push-ups and pull-ups. The key to effective strength training is to gradually increase the weight or resistance used in each exercise in order to continuously challenge the muscles and encourage growth.

In addition to building muscle mass, strength training has a number of other health benefits. For example, it can help to improve bone density, which is particularly important for women who are at risk for osteoporosis. It can also help to boost metabolism and promote weight loss, as muscle tissue burns more calories than fat tissue.

One important aspect of strength training is proper technique and form. It is important to use proper form in order to avoid injury and ensure that the exercises are targeting the intended muscle groups. Working with a certified personal trainer or strength training coach can be helpful in learning proper techniques and designing a safe and effective strength training program.

Incorporating strength training into your overall fitness routine can help to improve your physical health, increase your strength and endurance, and boost your confidence and self-esteem.

3. Flexibility Training

Flexibility training is an essential component of any well-rounded fitness routine. It involves stretching and lengthening muscles and joints to improve the range of motion and prevent injuries. Flexibility training can also promote relaxation, reduce stress, and improve overall physical performance.

There are several types of flexibility training, including static stretching, dynamic stretching, and proprioceptive neuromuscular facilitation (PNF) stretching.

Static stretching involves holding a stretch position for a prolonged period of time, usually around 30 seconds. It is often used after a workout to improve flexibility and prevent muscle soreness. Common static stretches include hamstring stretches, calf stretches, and shoulder stretches.

Dynamic stretching involves moving the body through a range of motion in a controlled and intentional manner. It is often used as a warm-up before a workout to prepare the muscles and joints for more intense activity. Examples of dynamic stretches include walking lunges, leg swings, and arm circles.

PNF stretching involves a combination of contracting and relaxing muscles to improve flexibility. It is often used in rehabilitation settings to improve range of motion and reduce muscle tension. PNF stretching is usually done with a partner or therapist who can provide resistance and assistance during the stretches.

Incorporating flexibility training into your fitness routine can be as simple as adding a few stretches at the end of your workout or doing a quick stretching routine in the morning. It's important to stretch all major muscle groups and to avoid bouncing or forcing stretches beyond what is comfortable.

Some tips for effective flexibility training include:

- **Start with a warm-up:** Before stretching, it's important to warm up your muscles with some light cardio or dynamic stretching to prevent injury.

- **Hold stretches for at least 30 seconds:** This allows the muscles to fully relax and lengthen.

- **Breathe deeply**: Breathing deeply and slowly can help relax the muscles and increase the effectiveness of the stretch.

- **Don't force the stretch:** Stretch only to the point of tension, not pain. Pushing too hard can cause injury.

- **Stretch regularly:** Flexibility training should be done at least 2-3 times per week to see results.

Incorporating flexibility training into your fitness routine can improve your overall health and well-being. By improving your range of motion and reducing muscle tension, you can move more easily, reduce your risk of injury, and feel more relaxed and comfortable in your body.

4.   High-Intensity Interval Training (HIIT)

High-Intensity Interval Training (HIIT) is a type of exercise that involves short bursts of intense activity alternated with periods of rest or low-intensity exercise. HIIT has gained popularity in recent years due to its efficiency and effectiveness in improving cardiovascular fitness and burning fat.

During a HIIT workout, the intensity of the exercise is usually around 80-95% of the maximum heart rate, which is higher than the intensity of traditional aerobic exercise. The intervals of high-intensity exercise can range from 20 seconds to 2 minutes, followed by periods of rest or low-intensity exercise that are typically equal to or longer in duration than the high-intensity intervals.

One of the main benefits of HIIT is that it can be done in a short amount of time. A typical HIIT workout can range from 10-30 minutes, making it a great option for those who are short on time but still want to get a good workout in. HIIT has been shown to be effective in improving cardiovascular health, increasing muscle mass, and reducing body fat.

Another benefit of HIIT is that it can be done with a variety of exercises, such as running, cycling, or bodyweight exercises, making it accessible to people of different fitness levels and preferences. However, it's important to gradually increase the intensity and duration of HIIT workouts to prevent injury.

Incorporating HIIT into a regular exercise routine can be a great way to improve cardiovascular fitness and overall health in a time-efficient manner.

Practical Tips for Incorporating Exercise into Daily Routines

Incorporating exercise into your daily routine can be challenging, but there are several practical tips that can help:

1. Find An Activity You Enjoy

Finding an activity you enjoy is one of the most important aspects of incorporating exercise into your daily routine. It can be challenging to stick to a workout plan if you dread the activity you have chosen. Instead of forcing yourself to do something you don't enjoy, try to find an exercise that you look forward to.

To begin, think about activities that you enjoy doing or that you have always wanted to try. Maybe you've always wanted to take a dance class or learn how to swim. Perhaps you love spending time outdoors, and hiking or biking could be a good fit for you. Alternatively, you may prefer more structured workouts like group fitness classes or weightlifting.

It's important to remember that exercise doesn't have to be limited to traditional workouts. Activities like gardening, playing with your kids, or walking your dog can also provide physical benefits. The key is to find something that gets you moving and that you enjoy doing.

Another helpful tip is to switch up your routine to prevent boredom. Try out different activities or mix up your workout with a variety of exercises. This can keep your workouts fresh and exciting, making it more likely that you will stick to your routine.

Lastly, don't be afraid to ask for help or seek out resources. Joining a fitness class or hiring a personal trainer can provide structure and accountability to your workout routine. You can also find workout plans or inspiration online through social media or fitness apps.

Incorporating exercise into your daily routine can be a challenge, but finding an activity you enjoy can make it much easier. Keep trying until you find the perfect fit for you, and don't forget to mix things up to prevent boredom. With dedication and consistency, regular exercise can become a rewarding and enjoyable part of your daily routine.

2. Set Realistic Goals

Setting realistic goals is an essential aspect of incorporating exercise into your daily routine. When setting goals, it is important to be realistic and specific about what you want to achieve. Instead of setting a vague goal like "I want to get in shape," try setting a specific and measurable goal like "I want to run a 5k in 3 months."

Once you have set your goals, it is important to create a plan of action. Break down your long-term goals into smaller, more manageable milestones. For example, if your goal is to run a 5k in 3 months, start with a goal of running for 10 minutes without stopping and gradually increase the time each week.

It's also important to track your progress. Keeping a log of your workouts and progress can help you stay motivated and see how far you've come. Additionally, don't be afraid to adjust your goals if you find that they are too easy or too challenging. Remember, the key is to set realistic and achievable goals that can help you maintain a consistent exercise routine over time.

3. Make It A Priority

Making exercise a priority is essential for incorporating it into your daily routine. It's easy to let other things take precedence over physical activity, but it's important to remember that exercise is not just about improving physical health but also mental health and productivity.

Here are some tips for making exercise a priority:

- **Schedule it:** Treat exercise like an important appointment by scheduling it into your calendar or planner. Make it non-negotiable and non-cancelable, just like any other important commitment.

- **Start small:** Don't overwhelm yourself by committing to an intense workout routine right away. Start with small goals like 10-15 minutes of activity per day and gradually increase the time and intensity.

- **Make it enjoyable:** Choose activities that you enjoy and look forward to. This will make it easier to stick with and will feel less like a chore.

- **Find an exercise buddy:** Working out with a friend or partner can make it more enjoyable and hold you accountable.

- **Celebrate your progress**: Celebrate your achievements along the way, whether it's hitting a new milestone or just consistently sticking with your exercise routine. This positive reinforcement can help keep you motivated and encouraged to continue.

4.   Find A Workout Partner

Having a workout partner can help you stay motivated and accountable in your fitness routine. You can find a partner among your friends, family members, or even colleagues at work. When you work out with a partner, you can push each other to achieve your fitness goals, provide encouragement and support, and make the workout more enjoyable.

Additionally, having a workout partner can help you stick to your exercise routine. When you know that someone is counting on you to show up, you are more likely to follow through on your commitment. Plus, having a workout partner can make exercise a social activity, which can help you look forward to your workouts and reduce feelings of boredom or loneliness that might occur when you work out alone.

When looking for a workout partner, it's important to find someone who has similar fitness goals and interests. This way, you can both benefit from the partnership and stay motivated. Additionally, you should choose someone who has a compatible schedule so that you can consistently work out together.

Finally, it's important to communicate with your workout partner and establish clear expectations about your fitness routine. This can include setting a regular workout schedule, determining which exercises you will do together, and establishing goals and milestones that you want to achieve together. By working together, you can stay on track and achieve your fitness goals.

5. Incorporate Exercise Into Your Daily Activities.

Incorporating exercise into your daily routine is a great way to ensure that you get some physical activity in, even when you're short on time. There are several ways to do this:

- **Walk or bike to work:** If your job is within walking or biking distance, consider leaving your car at home and getting some exercise on your way to work. This is a great way to start your day off with some physical activity and can also help reduce your carbon footprint.

- **Take the stairs:** Whenever possible, take the stairs instead of the elevator or escalator. This is an easy way to incorporate some extra exercise into your daily routine.

- **Do squats or lunges while brushing your teeth:** While you're brushing your teeth, try doing some squats or lunges. This will not only help you get some exercise in, but it will also make your teeth-brushing routine a bit more interesting.

- **Stand up and move around during commercial breaks:** If you're watching TV, use the commercial breaks as an opportunity to get up and move around. You could do some stretches, walk around the room, or do some quick exercises.

- **Do a quick workout before bed:** Before you go to bed, consider doing a quick workout. This could include some stretching, yoga, or bodyweight exercises. Not only will this help you get some physical activity in, but it can also help you unwind and relax before sleep.

Incorporating exercise into your daily routine doesn't have to be complicated or time-consuming. By finding ways to sneak in some physical activity throughout the day, you can improve your physical health and well-being without having to sacrifice other important commitments in your life.

Nutrition

The foods we eat have a significant impact on our physical health and overall well-being. A healthy, balanced diet can help us maintain a healthy weight, improve our energy levels, and reduce our risk of chronic diseases such as heart disease, diabetes, and cancer.

Here are some key principles of a healthy diet:

1.   Eat A Variety of Nutrient-Dense Foods

Eating a variety of nutrient-dense foods is an essential aspect of maintaining optimal physical health. Nutrient-dense foods are those that contain a high concentration of vitamins, minerals, and other important nutrients relative to their caloric content. By incorporating a diverse array of nutrient-dense foods into your diet, you can ensure that your body is receiving the nutrients it needs to function properly.

One of the best ways to ensure that you are eating a variety of nutrient-dense foods is to include a wide range of fruits and vegetables in your diet. Fruits and vegetables are rich in vitamins, minerals, fiber, and antioxidants, which help protect your body against disease and support healthy bodily functions. Aim to include a variety of colorful fruits and vegetables in your diet, such as leafy greens, berries, citrus fruits, carrots, and peppers.

In addition to fruits and vegetables, other nutrient-dense foods to include in your diet include lean proteins, whole grains, and healthy fats. Lean proteins, such as chicken, fish, and tofu, provide essential amino acids that support muscle growth and repair. Whole grains, such as brown rice and quinoa, are rich in fiber, vitamins, and minerals and can help regulate blood sugar levels. Healthy fats, such as those found in nuts, seeds, and avocados, provide important nutrients, and help maintain healthy brain function.

It is also important to limit or avoid processed and junk foods, which tend to be high in calories, sugar, and unhealthy fats. These foods can contribute to weight gain and increase your risk of developing chronic diseases such as diabetes, heart disease, and cancer.

By focusing on a variety of nutrient-dense foods and limiting unhealthy options, you can provide your body with the nutrients it needs to function at its best and maintain optimal physical health.

2. Limit Processed and High-Sugar Foods

Maintaining a healthy and balanced diet is essential for good physical health. In order to boost physical health and productivity, it is important to limit processed and high-sugar foods. Processed foods often contain high levels of salt, sugar, and unhealthy fats, which can contribute to weight gain, high blood pressure, and other health problems. High-sugar foods, such as candy, soda, and baked goods, can cause spikes in blood sugar levels and contribute to the development of chronic diseases such as type 2 diabetes.

To limit processed and high-sugar foods, it is important to read food labels carefully and avoid products that contain high amounts of added sugars, sodium, and unhealthy fats. Instead, choose whole, nutrient-dense foods such as fruits, vegetables, lean proteins, and whole grains. These foods provide essential vitamins and minerals that are necessary for good health and can help you maintain a healthy weight.

It can be challenging to limit processed and high-sugar foods, as they are often readily available and can be convenient for on-the-go meals. However, making a conscious effort to choose healthier options can have a significant impact on your overall health and wellbeing. This can include meal planning and preparation, packing healthy snacks, and making informed choices when eating out or buying pre-packaged foods.

By limiting processed and high-sugar foods and incorporating nutrient-dense options into your diet, you can improve your physical health, maintain a healthy weight, and increase your energy levels, allowing you to be more productive and focused throughout the day.

3. Stay Hydrated

Staying hydrated is an essential component of maintaining optimal physical health. The human body is composed of about 60% water, and staying hydrated ensures that our bodies can function properly. When we exercise, we lose water through sweat, and when we don't replace that lost water, we can become dehydrated, which can lead to fatigue, muscle cramps, and other health problems.

It is recommended that adults drink at least 8-10 glasses of water per day, but this can vary depending on individual needs and activity levels. Athletes and individuals who exercise regularly may need to consume more water to replace the water lost through sweat. Additionally, consuming foods with high water content, such as fruits and vegetables, can also contribute to overall hydration.

Aside from water, other beverages such as herbal teas, coconut water, and low-fat milk can also contribute to hydration. However, it is important to limit the consumption of sugary drinks, as they can have negative effects on overall health and contribute to weight gain.

Incorporating hydration into daily routines can be simple. Keeping a water bottle with you at all times can serve as a reminder to drink water throughout the day. Additionally, consuming water-rich foods like fruits and vegetables can also help maintain hydration levels.

4.   Practice Portion Control

Nutrition plays a critical role in overall health and fitness. While it is important to eat a variety of nutrient-dense foods, it is also important to practice portion control. Eating too much, even healthy foods, can lead to weight gain and other health issues. Here are some tips for practicing portion control:

- **Use smaller plates:** Research has shown that using smaller plates can help reduce the amount of food we eat. This is because our brain perceives a full plate as a full meal, regardless of the plate size.

- **Measure your food:** Use measuring cups and spoons to measure your food portions. This can be especially helpful for foods like pasta, rice, and cereal, which can be easy to overeat.

- **Pay attention to serving sizes:** Check the nutrition labels on packaged foods to see what a serving size is. This can help you understand how much you should be eating.

- **Eat slowly:** It takes time for our brain to register that we are full. Eating slowly and savoring each bite can help you feel more satisfied with less food.

- **Avoid distractions:** Eating while watching TV or using your phone can make it harder to pay attention to how much you are eating. Try to eat in a calm environment without distractions.

By practicing portion control, you can enjoy a variety of foods while still maintaining a healthy weight and overall health.

5.   Listen To Your Body

When it comes to nutrition, it's important to focus not only on what you eat but also on how you eat. One important aspect is listening to your body's hunger and fullness cues. Many people have lost touch with their body's natural signals due to a variety of factors such as busy schedules, emotional eating, or dieting.

To practice listening to your body, it's helpful to eat slowly and mindfully. Pay attention to the taste, texture, and aroma of your food. Take breaks between bites to check in with your hunger levels. Are you still hungry? Or are you starting to feel satisfied? Eating slowly and mindfully can help you tune in to your body's signals and prevent overeating.

Additionally, it's important to recognize that everyone's body is different and has different nutritional needs. Some people may thrive on a vegetarian or vegan diet, while others may require more protein and animal products. It's important to pay attention to how different foods make you feel and adjust your diet accordingly. Experiment with different foods and eating patterns to find what works best for your body.

Listening to your body is an important part of a healthy and balanced approach to nutrition. By paying attention to your body's hunger and fullness cues and experimenting with different foods, you can create a diet that supports your overall health and well-being.

6.   Avoid Restrictive Diets

When it comes to improving physical health, it's important to remember that nutrition plays a critical role. While many diets and nutrition plans may promise quick results, it's important to avoid overly restrictive diets that can do more harm than good. Restrictive diets can deprive the body of essential nutrients and may lead to long-term health problems.

Instead of following a restrictive diet, focus on making sustainable changes to your eating habits. This may include incorporating more fruits, vegetables, and whole grains into your diet, as well as reducing your intake of processed foods, added sugars, and saturated fats. It's also important to listen to your body and eat when you're hungry rather than depriving yourself of food.

In addition to improving physical health, a balanced and sustainable diet can also improve mental health and overall well-being. By focusing on nourishing your body with healthy foods, you can feel more energized, focused, and motivated to continue making positive changes in your life.

7. Be Mindful of Food Choices

Being mindful of food choices means paying attention to what you eat and making intentional decisions about what you put into your body. It involves being aware of the nutritional value of foods and making choices that align with your health goals.

One way to be more mindful of food choices is to plan ahead. Take time to make a grocery list and plan out your meals for the week. This can help you avoid impulse purchases and ensure that you have healthy options readily available. Additionally, you can try to cook at home more often instead of eating out or relying on processed foods.

Another aspect of being mindful of food choices is paying attention to how different foods make you feel. Some people may feel better when they eat a higher protein diet, while others may do better with more complex carbohydrates. It's important to listen to your body and make adjustments based on what works best for you.

It's also helpful to avoid distractions while eating, such as watching TV or working on the computer. Instead, take the time to enjoy your meals and savor the flavors and textures of the food.

Finally, it's important to remember that being mindful of food choices doesn't mean indulging in treats or "unhealthy" foods. It's about finding a balance and making intentional choices that support your overall health and well-being.

Incorporating these principles into your diet can have a significant impact on your physical health. It's also important to remember that everyone's nutritional needs are different, and consulting with a healthcare professional or registered dietitian can be helpful in developing a personalized nutrition plan.

Sleep

Sleep is an essential aspect of overall health and well-being. It is the time when the body repairs and rejuvenates itself, both physically and mentally. Lack of adequate sleep can lead to a host of health problems, including impaired cognitive function, mood disorders, and increased risk of chronic diseases such as diabetes and heart disease.

Adults typically need seven to nine hours of sleep per night, but individual needs may vary. Establishing a consistent sleep routine and creating a comfortable sleep environment can improve the quality and quantity of sleep. Here are some tips for optimizing sleep:

1.   Stick To A Regular Sleep Schedule

Sticking to a regular sleep schedule is an important aspect of promoting healthy sleep habits. It involves going to bed and waking up at the same time every day, even on weekends and holidays. By maintaining a consistent sleep schedule, your body's internal clock will be better able to regulate your sleep-wake cycle, resulting in more restful and rejuvenating sleep.

The first step to establishing a regular sleep schedule is to determine how much sleep you need. Adults typically require 7-9 hours of sleep per night, while children and teenagers require more.

Once you've determined how much sleep you need, you can work backward from your desired wake-up time to establish a consistent bedtime.

It's important to be consistent with your sleep schedule as much as possible, even on weekends and holidays. Sleeping in on the weekends may feel like a treat, but it can disrupt your body's internal clock and make it harder to fall asleep and wake up during the week. If you do need to deviate from your regular sleep schedule, try to limit the difference to no more than an hour or two.

To help establish a regular sleep schedule, try setting a consistent bedtime routine. This can include winding down with a relaxing activity like reading or taking a bath and avoiding stimulating activities like watching TV or using electronic devices in the hour leading up to bedtime. Creating a calming sleep environment, such as keeping your bedroom cool and dark, can also help promote a restful night's sleep.

By sticking to a regular sleep schedule, you can improve the quality and duration of your sleep, leading to a more energized and productive day.

2. Create A Relaxing Sleep Environment

Creating a relaxing sleep environment can greatly improve the quality and duration of your sleep. It involves creating a physical and mental space that promotes relaxation and calmness. Here are some tips for creating a relaxing sleep environment:

- **Make your bedroom comfortable:** Your bedroom should be comfortable and conducive to sleep. Invest in a good quality mattress and pillows that support your body and help you feel relaxed. Use soft and comfortable beddings that are soothing to the skin. Make sure the temperature of the room is cool and comfortable.

- **Reduce noise and light:** Noise and light can disrupt your sleep. Use earplugs or a white noise machine to block out unwanted noise. Use blackout curtains or an eye mask to keep the room dark and help your body produce melatonin, the hormone that regulates sleep.

- **Keep the room clutter-free:** A cluttered room can make it difficult to relax and fall asleep. Keep your bedroom clean and organized. Remove any distractions such as televisions, electronic gadgets, or work-related items from your bedroom.

- **Use aromatherapy:** Aromatherapy can help to create a relaxing environment that promotes sleep. Use the lavender essential oil or other relaxing scents in a diffuser to promote relaxation and calmness.

- **Practice relaxation techniques:** Practicing relaxation techniques such as deep breathing, meditation, or progressive muscle relaxation can help you feel relaxed and calm before bedtime. These techniques can help to reduce stress and anxiety, allowing you to fall asleep faster and enjoy better quality sleep.

By creating a relaxing sleep environment, you can help your body to relax and prepare for a restful night's sleep. It's important to establish a relaxing sleep routine and stick to it consistently to help your body and mind adjust to a healthy sleep pattern.

3. Limit Exposure To Screens

Getting enough high-quality sleep is crucial for maintaining physical health, mental well-being, and productivity. One of the key factors in achieving restful sleep is limiting exposure to screens, including smartphones, laptops, tablets, and televisions.

The blue light emitted by these devices can interfere with the body's natural sleep cycle by suppressing the production of melatonin, a hormone that regulates sleep. This can make it difficult to fall asleep and result in poor sleep quality. Additionally, the content of what you are viewing on these screens can also impact your mood and stress levels, leading to increased mental and physical arousal that can make it challenging to relax and fall asleep.

To create a more conducive sleep environment, it's recommended to limit screen time at least 30 minutes before bedtime. Instead, try relaxing activities such as reading a book, practicing meditation or gentle yoga, or taking a warm bath.

If you must use electronic devices before bed, consider installing blue light filters or using apps that can reduce blue light exposure.

In addition to limiting screen time before bed, it's also essential to create a comfortable and relaxing sleep environment. This may include keeping the bedroom cool, dark, and quiet, investing in comfortable bedding and pillows, and minimizing distractions such as noise or light. By creating a restful sleep environment and limiting exposure to screens, you can improve the quality and duration of your sleep, leading to better overall health and well-being.

4. Avoid Caffeine And Alcohol

Getting a good night's sleep is essential for physical health, and avoiding caffeine and alcohol before bedtime is one way to help achieve this. Both caffeine and alcohol can interfere with the quality of sleep.

Caffeine is a stimulant that can make it difficult to fall asleep and can also cause wakefulness during the night. It is best to avoid caffeine for at least four to six hours before bedtime. This means limiting coffee, tea, soda, and chocolate consumption in the evening. Some people are more sensitive to caffeine than others, so it's important to pay attention to how it affects you personally.

Alcohol, on the other hand, is a depressant that can make you feel drowsy and fall asleep faster. However, it can also lead to disrupted sleep patterns, frequent waking during the night, and less restful sleep overall. It is recommended to avoid alcohol at least three to four hours before bedtime to give your body enough time to metabolize it.

Avoiding caffeine and alcohol before bedtime can help you fall asleep faster, improve the quality of your sleep, and wake up feeling more rested and refreshed.

5.   Practice Relaxation Techniques

Getting enough quality sleep is essential for maintaining optimal physical health and productivity. However, sometimes it can be challenging to fall asleep or stay asleep. One way to overcome this is to practice relaxation techniques before bedtime.

There are many relaxation techniques that you can try, such as deep breathing exercises, progressive muscle relaxation, and visualization. These techniques can help reduce stress, anxiety, and tension, allowing you to enter a more relaxed state of mind and body, making it easier to fall asleep and stay asleep.

▪ Deep Breathing Exercises

Deep breathing exercises are a simple yet effective relaxation technique that can help calm the mind and prepare the body for sleep. They involve taking slow, deep breaths in through the nose and out through the mouth, with a focus on filling the lungs completely and exhaling fully.

To practice deep breathing exercises, find a quiet and comfortable place to sit or lie down. Close your eyes and take a few normal breaths to settle in. Then, inhale slowly and deeply through your nose, feeling your lungs fill with air and your belly expand. Hold your breath for a few seconds, then exhale slowly and completely through your mouth, feeling your belly deflate and your body relax. Repeat this cycle for several minutes, focusing on the sensations of the breath and allowing any thoughts or distractions to simply pass by.

Deep breathing exercises can be practiced at any time of day but are especially helpful before bed to calm the mind and prepare the body for sleep. They can also be combined with other relaxation techniques, such as guided imagery or progressive muscle relaxation, for a more comprehensive relaxation practice.

With regular practice, deep breathing exercises can become a powerful tool for promoting better sleep and overall health.

- **Progressive Muscle Relaxation**

Progressive muscle relaxation is a technique that involves tensing and relaxing different muscle groups in the body to promote physical and mental relaxation. The technique can be done in a seated or lying down position, with the eyes closed or open.

To start, focus on tensing the muscles in one specific area of the body, such as the feet or hands. Hold the tension for several seconds, then release and relax the muscles. Take a few deep breaths and focus on the feeling of relaxation in the muscles. Then, move on to another area of the body and repeat the process.

Progressive muscle relaxation can help reduce muscle tension and improve overall relaxation, making it a useful technique for promoting better sleep. It can also be helpful for managing anxiety, stress, and chronic pain. With regular practice, progressive muscle relaxation can become a valuable tool in managing physical and emotional well-being.

- **Visualization**

Visualization is a powerful technique that can help you relax and fall asleep more easily. It involves using your imagination to create a peaceful and calming image in your mind. This image can be anything that helps you feel relaxed and at ease, such as a beautiful beach, a quiet forest, or a peaceful garden.

To practice visualization, find a comfortable position in bed and close your eyes. Take a few deep breaths and focus on relaxing your body. Then, imagine yourself in a peaceful setting. Visualize the details of the scene and engage your senses – what do you see, hear, feel, and smell? Allow yourself to fully immerse in the scene and let any worries or stresses fade away.

It can be helpful to repeat a calming phrase or affirmation to yourself as you visualize, such as "I am calm and peaceful" or "I release all tension and stress." You can also try guided visualizations, which are available in the form of audio recordings or apps.

Visualization is a simple and effective relaxation technique that can be used at any time, not just at bedtime. With practice, it can help you feel more calm and centered and improve the quality of your sleep.

Incorporating relaxation techniques into your bedtime routine can help promote better sleep, leading to improved physical health and productivity.

Exercise Regularly

Regular exercise is a crucial component of maintaining good physical health and can also have a positive impact on sleep. Exercise helps to reduce stress, anxiety, and depression, which are common causes of sleep problems. It also helps to regulate the body's internal clock, making it easier to fall asleep at night and wake up in the morning.

However, it's important to note that the timing of exercise can affect sleep quality. While exercising earlier in the day can help promote better sleep, engaging in vigorous physical activity close to bedtime may interfere with sleep. This is because exercise increases heart rate and body temperature, making it harder to fall asleep.

In addition to timing, the type of exercise may also impact sleep quality. Research suggests that moderate-intensity aerobic exercise, such as brisk walking, running, or cycling, can improve sleep quality and duration. Resistance training, such as weight lifting, may also improve sleep quality.

It's important to consult with a healthcare professional before starting any new exercise routine, especially if you have any underlying medical conditions. Additionally, it's important to listen to your body and not overexert yourself, as this can lead to increased stress and negatively impact sleep quality.

Avoid Large Meals and Fluids Before Bedtime

Avoiding large meals and fluids before bedtime is another important aspect of improving sleep quality. Eating a heavy meal close to bedtime can cause discomfort and make it difficult to fall asleep. Similarly, drinking too much fluid before bed can increase the likelihood of needing to wake up to use the bathroom during the night.

It is recommended to finish eating meals at least two to three hours before bedtime and to limit fluid intake in the hours leading up to sleep. If you do feel hungry or thirsty before bed, choose a light snack, such as a piece of fruit or a small serving of yogurt, and drink only small amounts of fluids.

By avoiding large meals and fluids before bedtime, you can help reduce the chances of discomfort and disruption to your sleep, leading to a more restful and restorative night's sleep.

By prioritizing sleep and following these tips, individuals can improve their physical health, cognitive function, and overall well-being.

Stress Management

Stress is an inevitable part of life, but it's important to manage it effectively to maintain overall health and well-being. Chronic stress can lead to a range of physical and mental health problems, including cardiovascular disease, digestive disorders, anxiety, and depression.

Fortunately, there are many effective strategies for managing stress. The key is to find the techniques that work best for you and incorporate them into your daily routine. Here are some tips for effective stress management:

1. Practice Mindfulness Meditation

In the world we live in, it can be easy to get lost in the hustle and bustle of everyday life, causing us to experience stress and anxiety. One way to combat this is by practicing mindfulness meditation. This technique involves focusing your attention on the present moment and accepting your thoughts, feelings, and bodily sensations without judgment.

Through mindfulness meditation, you can learn to become more aware of your thoughts and emotions, allowing you to better manage them when they become overwhelming. It can also help you to become more relaxed and calm, which can have a positive impact on your physical health.

To begin practicing mindfulness meditation, find a quiet place where you won't be interrupted for a few minutes. Sit comfortably with your back straight, and close your eyes. Focus on your breathing, and try to keep your attention on the sensation of the air moving in and out of your body.

If your mind starts to wander, gently bring your focus back to your breath. You can also try focusing your attention on different parts of your body, such as your hands or feet, and notice any sensations you may be feeling.

Over time, with consistent practice, you may find that you are able to better manage stress and anxiety in your daily life. Mindfulness meditation can be a powerful tool to help you achieve optimal health and productivity.

2. Exercise Regularly

Exercise has been shown to be an effective way to manage stress and improve physical health. Regular exercise can help reduce stress hormones such as cortisol and adrenaline while also releasing endorphins, which are natural mood-boosting chemicals in the brain. Exercise can also improve sleep quality, which can further help reduce stress and improve overall well-being.

The type and duration of exercise that is best for stress management may vary depending on the individual's preferences and physical abilities. Some people may prefer aerobic exercises such as running or cycling, while others may prefer more calming exercises such as yoga or Tai Chi. A combination of both aerobic and calming exercises may be ideal for optimal stress management.

The recommended amount of exercise for adults is at least 150 minutes of moderate-intensity aerobic exercise per week or 75 minutes of vigorous-intensity aerobic exercise per week. Strength training exercises should also be done at least twice a week.

It's important to find an exercise routine that is enjoyable and sustainable, as consistency is key for long-term stress management and overall health. If someone is new to exercise, it may be helpful to start with shorter, easier workouts and gradually increase the duration and intensity over time. It may also be beneficial to incorporate exercise into one's daily routine, such as taking a walk during a lunch break or doing yoga before bed.

Regular exercise can be an effective and accessible tool for managing stress and improving physical health.

3. Get Enough Sleep

Getting enough sleep is crucial for managing stress. Lack of sleep can cause irritability, moodiness, and increased anxiety, making it more difficult to cope with stress. In addition, sleep deprivation can weaken the immune system and lead to physical health problems, which can exacerbate stress.

To get enough sleep, it is important to follow healthy sleep habits. This includes sticking to a regular sleep schedule, creating a relaxing sleep environment, limiting exposure to screens, avoiding caffeine and alcohol before bedtime, and practicing relaxation techniques before sleep. By incorporating these habits into your routine, you can improve the quality and quantity of your sleep, leading to better stress management and overall health.

4. Practice Relaxation Techniques

When you are feeling stressed, it can be helpful to have a few techniques in your arsenal that you can turn to in order to help calm your mind and body. There are many different relaxation techniques that you can try, and finding the ones that work best for you may take some trial and error. Some popular techniques include deep breathing exercises, progressive muscle relaxation, and visualization.

Deep breathing exercises involve taking slow, deep breaths in through your nose and out through your mouth. This technique can help to slow your heart rate, lower your blood pressure, and calm your mind. To practice deep breathing, find a quiet and comfortable space to sit or lie down. Close your eyes and focus on your breath, taking slow and deep breaths in through your nose and out through your mouth.

Progressive muscle relaxation involves tensing and relaxing

different muscle groups in your body, one at a time. This technique can help to release tension and promote relaxation throughout your body. To practice progressive muscle relaxation, find a quiet and comfortable space to sit or lie down. Close your eyes and focus on your breath. Starting with your toes, tense the muscles in that area of your body for a few seconds, then release and relax the muscles completely. Move up your body, tensing and relaxing each muscle group in turn.

Visualization involves creating a mental image of a peaceful and relaxing scene. This technique can help to distract your mind from stress and promote feelings of calm and relaxation. To practice visualization, find a quiet and comfortable space to sit or lie down. Close your eyes and focus on your breath. Then, create a mental image of a peaceful and relaxing scene. This could be a beach, a mountain top, or any other location that you find calming and peaceful. Try to engage all of your senses in this visualization, imagining the sights, sounds, and smells of your peaceful scene.

Overall, practicing relaxation techniques can help to promote feelings of calm and reduce stress. By incorporating these techniques into your daily routine, you can build resilience and improve your ability to manage stress effectively.

5. Engage in Activities You Enjoy

Engaging in activities that you enjoy is an important part of managing stress and promoting overall well-being. When you engage in activities that you enjoy, you give yourself a break from the stressors of daily life and allow yourself to experience positive emotions. This can help to reduce stress levels, promote relaxation, and improve your mood.

The activities that you choose to engage in should be ones that you find enjoyable, and that help you to relax. This could include things like reading a book, listening to music, gardening, cooking, playing sports, or spending time with loved ones. The key is to choose activities that you find fulfilling and that allows you to disconnect from your stressors.

When you engage in activities that you enjoy, it can also help you to build a sense of accomplishment and purpose. This can be particularly important if you are experiencing stress related to work or other responsibilities. By engaging in activities that you find fulfilling, you can give yourself a sense of achievement outside of your daily responsibilities.

It can be helpful to schedule regular time for activities that you enjoy. This can help you to prioritize these activities and ensure that you are making time for them in your busy schedule. You might also consider trying new activities or hobbies that you have always wanted to try, as this can help to keep things interesting and engaging.

Remember, managing stress is not just about reducing the negative impact of stressors but also about promoting positive emotions and experiences. By engaging in activities that you enjoy, you can help to improve your overall well-being and resilience in the face of stressors.

6.   Set Realistic Goals

Setting realistic goals is an important aspect of stress management. When you set realistic goals, you are more likely to accomplish them, which can help to reduce stress and anxiety.

It's important to remember that setting unrealistic goals can actually increase stress levels, as it creates pressure and expectations that are difficult to meet. When you set goals that are too high, you may feel like a failure if you don't achieve them, which can lead to negative self-talk and even more stress.

On the other hand, setting achievable goals can give you a sense of accomplishment and help to build confidence. When you meet a goal, no matter how small, it can provide a positive boost to your mood and motivation.

To set realistic goals, it's important to consider your current abilities, resources, and time constraints. You should also consider the level of difficulty of the goal and whether it is in alignment with your values and priorities.

Breaking larger goals down into smaller, more manageable steps can also be helpful. This can help you to track progress and maintain motivation, as each step brings you closer to achieving your ultimate goal.

Overall, setting realistic goals can be a powerful tool in managing stress and improving overall well-being. By setting goals that are achievable and in alignment with your values, you can reduce stress and build confidence in your abilities.

7. Seek Support

In our daily lives, stress can be a constant companion, and it can be challenging to manage it on our own. It is important to remember that seeking support is a sign of strength, and it can help us to cope better with stress.

Here are some ways to seek support:

- **Talk To A Trusted Friend or Family Member**

Talking to a trusted friend or family member is a valuable way to seek support when dealing with stress. Having someone to talk to can help you to feel less alone and provide a fresh perspective on your problems. It is important to choose someone you trust and feel comfortable opening up to.

When talking to a friend or family member about your stress, it is important, to be honest and clear about what you are going through. It can be helpful to share specific situations that are causing you stress, as well as any physical or emotional symptoms you may be experiencing.

It is also important to listen to your friend or family member's perspective and advice. They may be able to offer helpful suggestions or simply provide a listening ear. Remember that their advice may not always be the best solution for you, but having someone to talk to can still be a valuable source of support.

If you find that talking to a friend or family member is not enough, or if you need additional support, consider seeking professional help from a therapist or counselor. They can provide specialized guidance and support for dealing with stress and other mental health issues.

- **Seek Professional Help**

Seeking professional help is an important step in managing stress. While friends and family members can be supportive, sometimes more specialized assistance is needed. If you are experiencing severe or chronic stress, or if your stress is interfering with your ability to function in your daily life, seeking professional help may be the best course of action.

There are many different types of professionals who can help with stress management, including therapists, counselors, and psychiatrists. These professionals can work with you to develop personalized strategies for managing stress, such as cognitive-behavioral therapy, mindfulness-based stress reduction, or medication management.

When seeking professional help for stress, it is important to find a provider who is experienced in treating stress-related issues and with whom you feel comfortable sharing your thoughts and feelings. You may also want to consider factors such as cost, location, and availability when choosing a provider.

Remember that seeking professional help for stress is not a sign of weakness but rather a proactive step towards taking control of your health and well-being.

- **Join A Support Group**

Joining a support group can be a great way to seek support when dealing with stress. Support groups consist of individuals who are going through similar experiences and can provide empathy, understanding, and a sense of community. These groups can be either in-person or online and may focus on a specific topic or issue.

When joining a support group, it is important to find one that is a good fit for your needs. You may want to consider the focus of the group, its location or meeting times, and the size of the group. It may be helpful to attend a few meetings before deciding if a particular group is right for you.

In a support group, you can share your experiences and feelings and listen to the experiences of others. This can help you feel less alone and more understood. You may also receive practical advice and coping strategies from others who have gone through similar experiences.

Some support groups may be led by a professional, such as a therapist or social worker, while others may be peer-led. Both types of groups can be beneficial, and it may depend on your personal preference.

Joining a support group can be a valuable tool for managing stress and improving overall well-being. It is important to remember that seeking support is a sign of strength and can lead to positive changes in your life.

- **Practice Self-Care**

In addition to seeking support from others, it's important to also practice self-care as a way of managing stress. Self-care involves taking deliberate and intentional actions to care for your physical, mental, and emotional well-being. It can include activities such as exercise, meditation, getting enough sleep, eating a healthy diet, and engaging in enjoyable hobbies or activities.

When you prioritize self-care, you are giving yourself permission to take a break from the demands of daily life and focus on your own needs. This can help to reduce feelings of overwhelm, anxiety, and burnout that can result from chronic stress. Additionally, practicing self-care can improve your overall sense of well-being, increase resilience to stress, and enhance your ability to cope with challenging situations.

One effective self-care practice is to set aside regular time for activities that help you relax and recharge.

This might include taking a warm bath, practicing yoga, reading a book, or spending time in nature. It's also important to make time for activities that bring you joy and fulfillment, such as spending time with loved ones or pursuing a creative hobby.

Remember, self-care is not a luxury but a necessity for maintaining good health and well-being. By prioritizing self-care, you can better manage stress, improve your overall health, and increase your ability to cope with life's challenges.

Remember, seeking support is a sign of strength, and it can help you manage stress and improve your overall well-being.

Stress management is an ongoing process. What works for one person may not work for another, so it's important to experiment with different techniques and find what works best for you. By incorporating these tips into your daily routine, you can effectively manage stress and improve overall health and well-being.

Chapter 6

ENHANCING PRODUCTIVITY

In this chapter, we will explore techniques to enhance productivity in all areas of life. We will discuss the following:

1. **Understanding Productivity:** In this section, we will explore what productivity means and why it is important. We will also discuss the different types of productivity and how they relate to overall well-being.

2. **Identifying Personal Productivity Traps:** This section will help you identify common productivity traps and how to avoid them. We will discuss how to overcome procrastination, distractions, and time-wasting activities.

3. **Time Management Strategies:** Time management is a critical aspect of productivity. In this section, we will explore different time management strategies, including creating schedules, setting priorities, and minimizing interruptions.

4. **Goal Setting**: Goals provide direction and motivation for productivity. This section will help you set realistic and achievable goals and create a plan to achieve them.

5. **Focus and Concentration**: In this section, we will discuss how to improve focus and concentration, including techniques such as mindfulness, meditation, and

visualization.

6. **Effective Communication:** Communication is essential for productivity, whether it's communicating with others or with yourself. This section will explore techniques for effective communication, including active listening and assertiveness.

7. **Delegation and Outsourcing:** Delegation and outsourcing are important tools for increasing productivity. In this section, we will discuss how to identify tasks that can be delegated or outsourced and how to do them effectively.

8. **Streamlining Processes:** In this section, we will explore how to streamline processes and increase efficiency, including techniques such as automation and technology.

9. **Continuous Learning and Improvement:** Learning and improving continuously is important for productivity and personal growth. This section will explore different ways to learn and improve, including reading, courses, and feedback.

Overall, this chapter will provide you with a comprehensive understanding of productivity and practical techniques to enhance it in all areas of your life.

Understanding Productivity

In this section, we will explore what productivity means and why it is important. We will also discuss the different types of productivity and how they relate to overall well-being.

Productivity can be defined as the measure of how effectively and efficiently we use our time and resources to accomplish our goals. It is not just about getting things done but about getting the right things done. It is important because it directly impacts our personal and professional success, satisfaction, and overall well-being.

There are different types of productivity, including personal productivity, professional productivity, and social productivity. Personal productivity relates to achieving our personal goals, such as improving our health or learning a new skill. Professional productivity relates to accomplishing our work-related tasks and goals, while social productivity pertains to contributing to society and making a positive impact on the world.

Enhancing productivity requires a holistic approach that considers the physical, mental, emotional, and spiritual aspects of our being. To achieve optimal productivity, it is essential to prioritize tasks, set realistic goals, manage time effectively, minimize distractions, and maintain focus.

One practical technique for enhancing productivity is to practice mindfulness, which involves paying attention to the present moment with openness, curiosity, and non-judgment. Mindfulness helps to reduce stress and improve focus, creativity, and decision-making. Meditation is another technique that can help to enhance productivity by reducing stress and improving mental clarity.

Another way to enhance productivity is to identify and eliminate time-wasting activities, such as excessive social media use or multitasking. It is also essential to take breaks and engage in activities that promote relaxation, such as taking a walk, practicing yoga, or listening to music.

In addition to these techniques, it is crucial to develop healthy habits that support productivity, such as getting enough sleep, eating a balanced diet, and exercising regularly. Engaging in activities that promote social connections and positive relationships can also enhance productivity by providing support, motivation, and accountability.

Enhancing productivity is essential for achieving our personal and professional goals, as well as contributing to society and living a fulfilling life. By practicing mindfulness, eliminating time-wasting activities, and developing healthy habits, we can optimize our productivity and enhance our well-being.

Identifying Personal Productivity Traps

This section will help you identify common productivity traps and how to avoid them. We will discuss how to overcome procrastination, distractions, and time-wasting activities.

In this section of the chapter, we will be exploring common productivity traps and how to avoid them. Many people struggle with productivity due to various reasons, such as procrastination, distractions, and time-wasting activities. Identifying these traps is the first step in overcoming them and becoming more productive.

Procrastination

Procrastination is one of the most common productivity traps. It is the act of delaying or postponing tasks, usually to the last minute, despite knowing that they need to be done. Procrastination can lead to stress, missed deadlines, and poor performance. To overcome procrastination, it is essential to understand the underlying reasons for it. Often, procrastination stems from fear of failure, perfectionism, or lack of motivation.

To avoid procrastination, you can:

1. **Break tasks into smaller, manageable chunks:** Large tasks can be overwhelming and lead to procrastination. Breaking them down into smaller, achievable tasks can make them less daunting and easier to accomplish.

2. **Set deadlines:** Setting deadlines for each task can help to keep

you accountable and motivated to complete them on time.

3. **Eliminate distractions:** Identify and remove any distractions that may be hindering your progress, such as social media or your phone.

Distractions

Distractions are another common productivity trap. They can come in various forms, such as notifications on your phone, emails, or colleagues interrupting you. Distractions can derail your productivity and make it challenging to complete tasks efficiently.

To avoid distractions, you can:

1. **Turn off notifications:** Turn off notifications on your phone or computer to avoid getting distracted by them.

2. **Schedule times for emails and messages:** Set specific times to check and respond to emails and messages to avoid interrupting your work.

3. **Use noise-cancelling headphones:** If you work in a noisy environment, consider using noise-cancelling headphones to block out distractions.

Time-wasting Activities

Time-wasting activities are another common productivity trap. They can include activities such as browsing social media, watching TV, or engaging in idle chatter. Time-wasting activities can be detrimental to productivity and should be avoided.

To avoid time-wasting activities, you can:

1. **Prioritize tasks:** Prioritize tasks based on their importance and urgency. This can help you to focus on the most critical

tasks and avoid wasting time on less important ones.

2. **Set boundaries:** Set boundaries for yourself and others to avoid getting caught up in time-wasting activities. For example, let colleagues know when you need to work on an important task and cannot be interrupted.

3. **Take breaks:** Taking breaks can actually increase productivity by providing an opportunity to rest and recharge. However, it is essential to set a time limit for breaks to avoid wasting too much time.

By identifying and avoiding common productivity traps, you can become more productive and accomplish more in less time.

Time Management Strategies

Time management is a critical aspect of productivity. In this section, we will explore different time management strategies, including creating schedules, setting priorities, and minimizing interruptions.

Time management is an essential skill for enhancing productivity in all areas of life. It involves the effective allocation and prioritization of time to accomplish goals and complete tasks efficiently. In this section, we will explore different time management strategies that can help individuals boost their productivity.

The first step in effective time management is creating a schedule. This involves breaking down tasks into smaller, manageable pieces and allocating time for each task. It is essential to set realistic goals and avoid overloading oneself with too many tasks. To create an effective schedule, it is important to consider one's natural rhythms and peak times of productivity. For example, some individuals may be more productive in the morning, while others may be more productive in the afternoon or evening.

Another critical aspect of time management is setting priorities. It is essential to identify the most important tasks and prioritize them accordingly. One way to do this is to use the Eisenhower Matrix, which categorizes tasks into four quadrants based on their urgency and importance. This method allows individuals to focus on the most critical tasks and avoid getting bogged down by less important ones.

Minimizing interruptions is also key to effective time management. Distractions such as social media, email, and phone notifications can quickly derail productivity. One way to minimize interruptions is to set aside specific times to check email and social media rather than constantly checking them throughout the day. Additionally, it can be helpful to establish clear boundaries with colleagues, friends, and family to avoid interruptions during focused work time.

In summary, time management is crucial for enhancing productivity. By creating schedules, setting priorities, and minimizing interruptions, individuals can optimize their use of time and achieve their goals more efficiently. It is important to remember that effective time management requires discipline and practice, but the rewards in terms of productivity and overall well-being are well worth the effort.

Goal Setting

Goals provide direction and motivation for productivity. This section will help you set realistic and achievable goals and create a plan to achieve them.

Goal setting is a critical aspect of productivity as it provides direction and motivation. In this section, we will discuss how to set realistic and achievable goals and create a plan to achieve them.

1. **Define your goals:** Start by defining your goals clearly. What do you want to achieve? Be specific, measurable, and time-bound. For example, instead of saying, "I want to be more productive," say, "I want to complete three major tasks every day for the next two weeks."

2. **Prioritize your goals:** Once you have defined your goals, prioritize them based on importance and urgency. This will help you focus on the most important tasks and avoid wasting time on less important ones.

3. **Create a plan:** Once you have prioritized your goals, create a plan to achieve them. Break down each goal into smaller, actionable steps, and assign a deadline to each step. This will make it easier to track progress and stay motivated.

4. **Monitor your progress:** Regularly monitor your progress toward your goals. This will help you identify areas where you need to make adjustments and stay motivated by seeing your progress over time.

5. **Celebrate your successes:** Celebrate your successes along the way, no matter how small they may seem. This will help you stay motivated and continue working towards your goals.

Practical techniques to enhance productivity in all areas of one's life include using a planner or calendar to schedule tasks, minimizing distractions such as social media and email notifications, and breaking tasks down into smaller, more manageable pieces. Additionally, mindfulness and meditation techniques can help improve focus and reduce stress, leading to increased productivity.

Focus and Concentration

In this section, we will discuss how to improve focus and concentration, including techniques such as mindfulness, meditation, and visualization.

In today's world, distractions are ubiquitous, and it can be difficult to maintain focus and concentration for extended periods. However, improving focus and concentration is crucial for enhancing productivity. In this section, we will discuss some practical techniques to improve focus and concentration.

One powerful technique to improve focus and concentration is mindfulness. Mindfulness is the practice of paying attention to the present moment in a non-judgmental way. When we are mindful, we can observe our thoughts, emotions, and sensations without getting carried away by them. This can help us stay focused on the task at hand and avoid getting distracted by irrelevant thoughts or stimuli.

Meditation is another technique that can improve focus and concentration. Meditation involves focusing on a single object, such as the breath, and maintaining that focus for an extended period. Through regular practice, we can strengthen our ability to concentrate and reduce the impact of distractions on our minds.

Visualization is another powerful technique to improve focus and concentration. Visualization involves creating mental images of the task we are trying to accomplish. For example, if we are writing an article, we can visualize ourselves sitting at the desk, typing away, and completing the article. This can help us stay focused and motivated.

In addition to these techniques, there are other practical strategies to enhance focus and concentration. One is to eliminate distractions as much as possible. This might involve turning off notifications on our phones, closing unnecessary tabs on our computers, or finding a quiet place to work. Another strategy is to break the task into smaller, manageable parts. This can make the task feel less overwhelming and help us stay focused on the next step.

Overall, improving focus and concentration is crucial for enhancing productivity. By incorporating techniques such as mindfulness, meditation, visualization, and practical strategies like eliminating distractions and breaking tasks into smaller parts, we can improve our ability to concentrate and achieve our goals more efficiently.

Effective Communication

Communication is essential for productivity, whether it's communicating with others or with yourself. This section will explore techniques for effective communication, including active listening and assertiveness.

Effective communication is a crucial aspect of productivity as it facilitates understanding, clarity, and cooperation among individuals. Whether it's communicating with colleagues, family members, or oneself, effective communication can help enhance productivity and prevent misunderstandings.

One essential technique for effective communication is active listening. Active listening involves paying attention to the speaker, maintaining eye contact, and providing feedback to demonstrate that you understand their message.

Active listening can help prevent miscommunication and increase understanding among individuals. It can also help individuals develop empathy, which is crucial for effective communication.

Another technique for effective communication is assertiveness. Assertiveness involves expressing oneself clearly and confidently while respecting the rights and opinions of others. Assertiveness can help individuals express their needs and goals effectively, leading to a better understanding of expectations and ultimately increasing productivity.

It's also essential to understand how to communicate with oneself effectively. Self-talk can have a significant impact on productivity and self-esteem. Negative self-talk can hinder productivity and cause stress, while positive self-talk can increase confidence and motivation. By practicing positive self-talk, individuals can enhance their productivity and overall well-being.

Finally, communication skills can be enhanced through mindfulness and meditation practices. Mindfulness and meditation can help individuals develop awareness and attention, which can lead to better communication skills. By practicing mindfulness and meditation regularly, individuals can improve their ability to communicate effectively and enhance their overall productivity.

Delegation and Outsourcing

Delegation and outsourcing are important tools for increasing productivity. In this section, we will discuss how to identify tasks that can be delegated or outsourced and how to do them effectively.

Delegation and outsourcing are key strategies for enhancing productivity, especially when it comes to managing time and focusing on the most important tasks. Delegation involves assigning tasks to others, while outsourcing involves hiring external individuals or companies to perform certain tasks. In this section, we will explore how to effectively delegate and outsource tasks to maximize productivity.

The first step in delegation is to identify tasks that can be delegated. It is important to assess your strengths and weaknesses and determine which tasks can be effectively handled by others. Tasks that are routine, time-consuming, or require specific expertise can often be delegated. It is important to communicate clearly with the person to whom you are delegating the task, providing clear instructions and setting expectations for deadlines and quality of work.

Outsourcing involves hiring individuals or companies outside of your organization to perform tasks. This can include tasks such as administrative work, marketing, or IT support. It is important to carefully assess potential vendors and ensure they have the expertise and capacity to handle the task effectively. In addition, clear communication and expectations are crucial to ensure the outsourced work meets your standards.

It is important to note that while delegation and outsourcing can be powerful tools for enhancing productivity, it is also important to maintain a level of oversight to ensure quality and timeliness. Effective delegation and outsourcing require clear communication, trust, and effective management.

In summary, delegation and outsourcing can help individuals and organizations increase productivity by allowing individuals to focus on their strengths and prioritize their time effectively. By identifying tasks that can be effectively handled by others, carefully communicating expectations and providing oversight, delegation and outsourcing can be effective strategies for enhancing productivity.

Streamlining Processes

In this section, we will explore how to streamline processes and increase efficiency, including techniques such as automation and technology.

Streamlining processes is a key aspect of enhancing productivity. When we streamline our processes, we increase efficiency and reduce wasted time and resources. In this section, we will explore some techniques to streamline processes, including automation and technology.

The first step in streamlining processes is to identify areas where we can eliminate unnecessary steps or reduce the time it takes to complete a task. This can be done by examining the steps involved in a process and identifying any areas that are redundant or inefficient. Once we have identified these areas, we can look for ways to streamline the process.

One way to streamline processes is through automation. Automation involves using technology to perform tasks automatically without the need for human intervention. For example, we can use software to automate repetitive tasks, such as data entry or report generation. This can save a significant amount of time and reduce the risk of errors.

Another way to streamline processes is through the use of technology. There are many tools and apps available that can help us manage our time and tasks more efficiently. For example, we can use project management software to organize tasks and deadlines, or we can use scheduling apps to manage our calendars and appointments.

In addition to automation and technology, there are other techniques that can help us streamline processes. For example, we can create templates for commonly used documents or emails, which can save time and reduce the need for repetitive typing. We can also batch similar tasks together, such as answering emails or making phone calls, to increase efficiency and reduce the need for context switching.

Overall, streamlining processes is an important aspect of productivity. By identifying areas where we can eliminate unnecessary steps or reduce the time it takes to complete a task and by using automation, technology, and other techniques, we can increase efficiency and reduce wasted time and resources. These practical techniques can be applied to all areas of one's life, including work and personal tasks.

Continuous Learning and Improvement

Learning and improving continuously is important for productivity and personal growth. This section will explore different ways to learn and improve, including reading, courses, and feedback.

Continuous learning and improvement are essential for achieving optimal productivity and personal growth. When we are open to learning new things and constantly seeking to improve ourselves, we become more efficient and effective in our work, and we grow as individuals. In this section, we will explore different ways to learn and improve, including reading, courses, and feedback, and provide practical techniques to enhance it in all areas of one's life.

Reading is a powerful tool for continuous learning and improvement. By reading books and articles on topics related to our work and interests, we can stay up-to-date on the latest trends and best practices. We can also learn from the experiences of others, gaining valuable insights that can help us improve our own performance.

Courses are another great way to learn and improve. Whether it's a formal course or an online tutorial, taking a course can provide us with structured learning that is tailored to our specific needs. Courses can also provide us with opportunities to interact with other learners, share ideas, and receive feedback.

Feedback is a crucial component of continuous learning and improvement. By seeking feedback from others, we can gain valuable insights into our strengths and weaknesses and identify areas where we need to improve. Feedback can also help us to identify blind spots and biases that may be limiting our performance.

In addition to these specific techniques, there are a few general principles that can help us to continuously learn and improve:

1. **Embrace a growth mindset:** A growth mindset is a belief that our abilities can be developed through hard work and

dedication. By adopting a growth mindset, we can approach challenges with a positive attitude, viewing them as opportunities to learn and grow.

2. **Set goals:** Setting clear and achievable goals can help us to focus our learning and improvement efforts. By setting goals that are specific, measurable, and time-bound, we can track our progress and celebrate our successes.

3. **Seek out mentors:** Mentors can provide us with guidance and support as we navigate our learning and improvement journeys. By finding mentors who are experienced in our fields, we can gain valuable insights and learn from their experiences.

In summary, continuous learning and improvement are crucial for achieving optimal productivity and personal growth. By embracing reading, courses, feedback, a growth mindset, goal-setting, and mentorship, we can develop our skills and knowledge, overcome our limitations, and reach our full potential.

Chapter 7

DEVELOPING POSITIVE HABITS

Importance of Developing Positive Habits

Habits are powerful tools that can help us achieve our goals, increase productivity, and improve our overall well-being. Developing positive habits is essential for creating positive change in our lives. In this section, we will explore the importance of developing positive habits, including:

1. Understanding the Nature of Habits

In this section, we will discuss what habits are, how they are formed, and how they can be changed. We will also explore the different types of habits, including good habits, bad habits, and neutral habits.

In order to develop positive habits, it's important to first understand the nature of habits themselves. Habits are routines or behaviors that we engage in repeatedly, often without conscious thought. They are deeply ingrained in our brains and can be difficult to break or change.

Habits are formed through a process called "habituation." This process occurs when we repeat a behavior in a consistent context, which creates neural pathways in our brains that make it easier for us to repeat that behavior in the future. This is why it's easier to form habits when we engage in the same behavior at the same time and in the same environment each day.

Habits can be positive or negative. Positive habits, such as exercising regularly, eating a healthy diet, and practicing mindfulness, can improve our physical and mental health, while negative habits, such as smoking, procrastination, and excessive drinking, can have harmful effects on our health and well-being.

It's important to note that habits are not the same as addictions. While habits can become ingrained in our brains and be difficult to break, addictions involve a psychological and physical dependence on a substance or behavior.

Understanding the nature of habits is important for developing positive habits because it allows us to recognize the power of habituation and the need for consistency and repetition in creating new habits. It also helps us to identify and break negative habits, which can be a significant obstacle to achieving our goals and living a healthy, productive life.

2. Benefits of Positive Habits

Developing positive habits has numerous benefits, such as increased productivity, better health, and greater happiness. We will explore these benefits in detail and discuss how positive habits can help us achieve our goals.

Positive habits can bring a wide range of benefits to our lives. Here are some of the most notable:

- **Improved health:** Developing positive habits such as regular exercise, healthy eating, and getting enough sleep can significantly improve our physical health. This, in turn, can lead to better overall well-being and a reduced risk of chronic illnesses.

- **Increased productivity:** Habits such as time management, goal-setting, and prioritizing tasks can help us be more productive and efficient. This can lead to greater success and accomplishment in both our personal and professional lives.

- **Reduced stress:** Habits such as mindfulness, meditation, and deep breathing exercises can help us manage stress and anxiety more effectively. This can lead to improved mental health and a greater sense of calm and relaxation.

- **Better relationships:** Positive habits such as effective communication, active listening, and showing gratitude can help us build stronger and more meaningful relationships with others. This can lead to greater social support and a sense of belonging.

- **Personal growth:** Habits such as continuous learning, self-reflection, and practicing gratitude can help us grow and develop as individuals. This can lead to greater self-awareness, confidence, and a sense of purpose in life.

Developing positive habits can bring numerous benefits to our lives and help us become the best versions of ourselves.

3. Identifying Negative Habits

Before we can develop positive habits, we must identify our negative habits. In this section, we will discuss how to identify negative habits and the impact they can have on our lives.

In order to develop positive habits, it is important to first identify and address negative habits that may be hindering personal growth and productivity. Negative habits can be defined as actions or behaviors that are detrimental to one's well-being and progress toward goals.

Identifying negative habits requires self-reflection and awareness. It is important to take a close look at daily routines and actions to determine which habits may be having a negative impact on overall well-being and productivity. Some common negative habits include procrastination, excessive social media use, unhealthy eating habits, lack of exercise, negative self-talk, and substance abuse.

Once negative habits are identified, it is important to address them in a proactive and constructive manner. This may involve setting goals and developing new positive habits to replace the negative ones. It may also involve seeking support from others, such as a therapist or accountability partner, to help overcome negative habits and develop new positive ones.

It is important to remember that developing positive habits is a process and may take time and effort. By identifying negative habits and taking proactive steps to address them, individuals can improve their overall well-being and increase their productivity in all areas of life.

4. Techniques For Developing Positive Habits

Once we have identified our negative habits, we can begin to develop positive habits. In this section, we will explore different techniques for developing positive habits, including habit stacking, setting SMART goals, and using positive reinforcement.

Developing positive habits can be challenging, but there are several techniques that can help make the process easier and more effective:

- **Start small:** Begin by identifying one small habit that you would like to develop, and focus on that habit until it becomes automatic. Once you have successfully developed one positive habit, you can then move on to developing other habits.

- **Set realistic goals:** It is important to set realistic goals when developing positive habits. Setting goals that are too challenging can be discouraging and may lead to giving up on the habit altogether. Start with small, achievable goals and gradually increase the difficulty as you progress.

- **Use positive reinforcement:** Positive reinforcement can be a powerful tool for developing positive habits. Reward yourself for making progress and achieving your goals, such as treating yourself to a favorite snack or activity.

- **Practice self-awareness:** Being aware of your habits and behaviors is key to developing positive habits. Take note of the habits you want to change and why, and track your progress over time.

- **Use mindfulness and meditation:** Mindfulness and meditation can help you become more aware of your thoughts, feelings, and behaviors. They can also help you stay focused and motivated while developing positive habits.

- **Surround yourself with support:** Surrounding yourself with supportive people can be incredibly helpful when developing positive habits. Share your goals with friends or family members who can offer encouragement and accountability.

- **Create a routine:** Developing a routine can help make positive habits more automatic. Try to do the habit at the same time every day, and make it part of your daily routine.

- **Practice consistency:** Consistency is key when developing positive habits. Make a commitment to practice the habit every day, even if it's just for a few minutes. Over time, this consistency will help the habit become automatic.

By incorporating these techniques into your life, you can develop positive habits that will help you achieve your goals and improve your overall well-being. Remember to be patient and persistent, as developing new habits takes time and effort.

5. Maintaining Positive Habits

Developing positive habits is not enough; we must also maintain them. In this section, we will discuss strategies for maintaining positive habits, including tracking progress, building accountability, and practicing self-compassion.

Maintaining positive habits can be a challenge, as it is easy to slip back into old, negative habits. However, there are several strategies that can be employed to help maintain positive habits and continue to build on them. Here are some techniques that can be useful:

- **Consistency:** Consistency is key when it comes to maintaining positive habits. It is important to establish a routine and stick to it as much as possible. This means setting aside specific times each day or week to practice the habit, even when other things come up.

- **Accountability:** Having someone to hold you accountable can be a powerful motivator. This could be a friend, family member, or even a coach or mentor who can provide support and encouragement.

- **Self-reflection:** Regularly reflecting on the progress made with the positive habit can help maintain motivation and focus. Take time to assess how the habit is working for you and make adjustments as needed.

- **Mindfulness and meditation:** Mindfulness and meditation can be helpful in maintaining positive habits by increasing awareness and reducing stress. These practices can also help with impulse control and decision-making, making it easier to resist negative habits.

- **Rewards:** Celebrating small successes along the way can help maintain motivation and reinforce positive habits. Rewarding yourself for sticking to the habit can also create a positive association with the habit and increase the likelihood of continuing it.

- **Avoid triggers:** Avoiding triggers that may lead to negative habits can be an effective way to maintain positive habits. This may mean avoiding certain environments or situations that could be tempting or finding alternative ways to deal with stress or boredom.

By implementing these techniques, it is possible to maintain positive habits and continue to build on them over time. Remember that developing positive habits is a process, and setbacks are normal. The important thing is to stay committed and keep moving forward.

6. Overcoming Obstacles

Developing positive habits is not always easy. In this section, we will discuss common obstacles to developing positive habits and techniques for overcoming them, including dealing with failure and setbacks, building resilience, and practicing self-care.

Overcoming obstacles is a crucial aspect of developing positive habits. It is common for individuals to encounter obstacles in the process of habit formation. Obstacles can take many forms, including external factors such as lack of time or resources, as well as internal factors such as negative self-talk or self-doubt. In this section, we will discuss common obstacles to developing positive habits and techniques for overcoming them.

Dealing with failure and setbacks is a key part of maintaining positive habits. It is normal to experience setbacks when trying to develop new habits. It is important to remember that setbacks do not define us or our ability to form positive habits. Rather, setbacks provide an opportunity to learn and grow. To overcome setbacks, we must learn to cultivate resilience, which involves the ability to adapt and recover from adversity.

Building resilience involves several techniques, including mindfulness and meditation. Mindfulness and meditation help us to be more aware of our thoughts and emotions and to develop a more compassionate and non-judgmental relationship with ourselves.

This allows us to approach setbacks with greater clarity and a more positive mindset. It also helps us to focus on the present moment and to avoid getting caught up in negative thoughts or worries about the future.

Another important aspect of overcoming obstacles is practicing self-care. Self-care involves taking care of our physical, emotional, and mental health. This can involve activities such as exercise, healthy eating, getting enough sleep, and taking breaks to rest and recharge. When we take care of ourselves, we are better able to face challenges and approach habit formation with a positive and proactive attitude.

In addition to mindfulness, meditation, resilience, and self-care, there are many other techniques that can help us to overcome obstacles in habit formation. These include setting realistic goals, seeking support from others, creating a supportive environment, and practicing positive self-talk. By incorporating these techniques into our daily lives, we can overcome obstacles and develop positive habits that support our health and well-being.

How Habits Can Impact Overall Health and Productivity

Habits are repetitive behaviors that we engage in regularly and automatically, often without conscious thought. These habits can have a significant impact on our overall health and productivity, both positively and negatively.

Positive habits, such as regular exercise, eating a healthy diet, and getting enough sleep, can lead to improved physical health, increased energy levels, and better mental clarity. These habits can also increase productivity by providing us with the energy and focus needed to tackle tasks more efficiently.

On the other hand, negative habits, such as smoking, excessive drinking, and a sedentary lifestyle, can have serious negative impacts on our health and productivity. These habits can lead to chronic health conditions, decreased energy levels, and impaired cognitive function. Negative habits can also lead to increased stress levels, which can further reduce productivity.

It's important to note that habits don't just impact our physical health and productivity but also our emotional well-being. Negative habits can lead to increased feelings of guilt, shame, and low self-esteem, which can further impair our ability to be productive.

By developing positive habits and breaking negative ones, we can significantly improve our overall health and productivity. This can be achieved through a combination of self-awareness, discipline, and commitment. With practice and persistence, positive habits can become automatic and effortless, leading to long-term benefits for both our physical and mental well-being.

Understanding Habits

What are Habits?

Habits are automatic patterns of behavior that we engage in repeatedly without much conscious thought or effort. They are actions or behaviors that have become second nature to us, often through repetition or routine. Habits can be both positive and negative, and they can have a significant impact on our overall health and productivity.

Habits are formed through a process known as habituation, which occurs when a behavior is repeated over time, and the neural pathways in the brain become strengthened. As these pathways become more ingrained, the behavior becomes more automatic and requires less conscious effort to perform.

Habits can be triggered by various cues or stimuli in our environment, such as time of day, location, emotions, or other people. Once the habit is triggered, it follows a routine or series of actions that result in a reward or outcome. This reward reinforces the behavior and strengthens the neural pathway associated with it.

In many cases, we are not even aware of our habits, as they have become so automatic and ingrained in our daily lives. However, by understanding the nature of habits and how they are formed, we can begin to develop new, positive habits that can improve our health and productivity.

How are Habits Formed?

Habits are formed through a process called habituation, which is the brain's way of learning and adapting to repetitive behaviors. When we repeatedly engage in a specific behavior, our brain creates neural pathways that make it easier and more automatic for us to perform that behavior in the future.

The process of habit formation involves three stages: the cue, the behavior, and the reward. The cue is a trigger that prompts the behavior, while the reward is the positive outcome that reinforces the behavior and increases the likelihood of it being repeated in the future.

For example, let's say someone wants to develop a habit of exercising every morning. The cue could be setting the alarm for the same time every day, which prompts the behavior of getting out of bed and putting on workout clothes. The reward could be the feeling of accomplishment and increased energy levels that come from completing a morning workout, which reinforces the behavior and increases the likelihood of repeating it in the future.

Over time, habits become more automatic and require less conscious effort to perform. This is why it can be difficult to break a bad habit or develop a new positive habit - because the neural pathways in our brain have already been formed and reinforced. However, with deliberate effort and practice, it is possible to change and improve our habits for the better.

The Habit Loop: Cue, Routine, Reward

The habit loop is a framework that explains how habits are formed and maintained. It consists of three components: the cue, the routine, and the reward.

The cue is the trigger or the prompt that initiates the habit. It can be anything from a specific time of day to a certain location or an emotional state. Cues can be external, such as seeing a food commercial on TV that triggers a craving, or internal, such as feeling anxious or stressed.

The routine is the behavior or action that follows the cue. It's the habit itself, whether it's eating a sugary snack, scrolling through social media, or going for a run. This behavior can be physical, mental, or emotional.

The reward is the positive outcome that reinforces the behavior and strengthens the habit. It can be the pleasure of eating something sweet, the feeling of connection and validation from social media, or the sense of accomplishment and endorphins from exercise.

Over time, the habit loop becomes automatic, and the behavior becomes a habit. The brain learns to associate the cue with the routine and the reward, and the habit becomes more and more ingrained. This can be positive or negative, depending on the habit.

By understanding the habit loop, we can become more aware of our own habits and work to change them. We can identify the cues that trigger our negative habits and replace them with positive cues that lead to healthy habits. We can also find new routines that give us similar rewards to our old habits but in a healthier way.

Overall, understanding the habit loop can help us to develop positive habits that support our health and productivity while breaking negative habits that hold us back.

The Role of the Brain in Habit Formation

The brain plays a crucial role in the formation of habits. Every time we engage in a particular behavior, a neural pathway is formed in the brain. The more we repeat the behavior, the stronger the neural pathway becomes. Eventually, the behavior becomes automatic and habitual, and we perform it without conscious thought.

One of the key regions of the brain involved in habit formation is the basal ganglia, which is responsible for voluntary motor movements and habit learning. When we perform a habit, the basal ganglia receive a cue from the environment and initiate the associated routine. Once the routine is complete, the basal ganglia receive a reward signal, which reinforces the behavior and strengthens the associated neural pathway.

The prefrontal cortex, located at the front of the brain, also plays a role in habit formation. This region is responsible for decision-making and planning, and it helps us to consciously develop new habits. When we first start to develop a new habit, the prefrontal cortex is heavily involved in consciously making the decision to perform the behavior and planning the associated routine. Over time, as the behavior becomes more automatic, the prefrontal cortex becomes less involved, and the habit is controlled more by the basal ganglia.

Research has also shown that the brain is capable of creating new neural pathways and rewiring existing ones throughout our lives, a process known as neuroplasticity. This means that we can intentionally cultivate new habits by repeating a behavior consistently over time and strengthening the associated neural pathway in our brain.

Overall, understanding the role of the brain in habit formation can help us to develop positive habits and break negative ones. By intentionally repeating a desired behavior and reinforcing it with a reward, we can strengthen the neural pathway associated with that behavior and make it a habit.

Types of Habits

Good Habits vs. Bad Habits

In our daily lives, we are constantly engaged in various activities and behaviors that contribute to our overall well-being and success. Some of these activities, such as regular exercise and healthy eating habits, have positive effects on our health and productivity, while others, such as procrastination and addiction, can have negative impacts.

Good habits are behaviors that contribute positively to our well-being and help us achieve our goals. They are often characterized by consistency and persistence, and they require effort and commitment to maintain. Examples of good habits include regular exercise, meditation, healthy eating, practicing gratitude, and good time management.

On the other hand, bad habits are behaviors that have negative impacts on our health, productivity, and overall well-being. They are often characterized by inconsistency, impulsivity, and lack of control. Examples of bad habits include procrastination, smoking, excessive drinking, overeating, and lack of exercise.

One of the key differences between good and bad habits is their effects on our brain and mental state. Good habits can lead to positive changes in our brain chemistry, leading to feelings of well-being and motivation, while bad habits can lead to negative changes in brain chemistry, leading to anxiety, depression, and other negative emotions.

Another important factor that distinguishes good habits from bad habits is their long-term effects on our health and well-being. Good habits tend to have long-lasting positive effects, while bad habits tend to have negative effects that accumulate over time and can lead to chronic health problems.

Developing good habits and breaking bad habits is a crucial step toward achieving optimal health and productivity. With the right mindset and strategies, it is possible to replace negative habits with positive ones, leading to a happier and more fulfilling life.

Health Habits

Developing and maintaining good health habits is crucial for achieving optimal health and well-being. These habits can include a range of activities, behaviors, and practices that contribute to physical, mental, and emotional wellness. In this section, we will explore some common health habits that can be incorporated into one's daily routine.

a. **Regular exercise**: Regular physical activity is essential for maintaining physical fitness and overall health. Exercise can help to reduce the risk of chronic diseases, improve cardiovascular health, boost mood and mental health, and enhance cognitive function. The recommended amount of physical activity varies depending on age and fitness level, but the general guideline is to aim for at least 30 minutes of moderate-intensity exercise most days of the week.

b. **Healthy eating**: A balanced and nutritious diet is essential for maintaining good health. This means consuming a variety of fruits, vegetables, whole grains, lean proteins, and healthy fats while limiting processed foods, added sugars, and saturated fats. Eating a healthy diet can help to maintain a healthy weight, reduce the risk of chronic diseases, and promote overall well-being.

c. **Good sleep habits**: Getting enough quality sleep is crucial for maintaining physical and mental health. Sleep plays a vital role in the body's restorative processes, helping to repair and rejuvenate tissues, regulate hormones, and consolidate memories. Developing good sleep habits, such as establishing a regular sleep schedule, limiting caffeine and alcohol intake, and creating a relaxing sleep environment, can help to improve sleep quality and duration.

d. **Stress management**: Chronic stress can have detrimental effects on physical and mental health, so it is important to develop effective stress management techniques. Mindfulness meditation, deep breathing exercises, and regular physical activity are all effective strategies for managing stress and promoting relaxation.

e. **Hydration:** Drinking enough water is essential for maintaining optimal health. Proper hydration can help to regulate body temperature, lubricate joints, and support organ function. The recommended amount of water varies depending on age, sex, and activity level, but the general guideline is to aim for at least 8 cups (64 ounces) of water per day.

By incorporating these healthy habits into one's daily routine, individuals can promote optimal health and well-being. It is important to remember that developing good health habits takes time and effort, but the benefits are well worth it.

Productivity Habits

Productivity habits refer to a set of practices and behaviors that help individuals accomplish more tasks and achieve their goals efficiently. These habits are essential for anyone who wants to succeed in their personal or professional life. By adopting effective productivity habits, individuals can manage their time more efficiently, minimize distractions, and maintain focus, which can significantly boost their productivity.

Here are some examples of productivity habits:

a. **Prioritizing**: One of the most effective productivity habits is prioritizing tasks. This involves determining which tasks are most important and need to be completed first. This helps individuals to focus their energy and resources on the most critical tasks.

b. **Time management**: Managing time effectively is another important productivity habit. This involves allocating time for each task and ensuring that it is completed within the allotted time. Time management skills help individuals to use their time wisely and avoid procrastination.

c. **Setting goals**: Productive individuals set clear and specific goals for themselves. By setting goals, they have a clear direction and purpose, which helps them to stay focused and motivated.

d. **Breaking tasks into smaller parts**: Large tasks can be overwhelming and lead to procrastination. Productive individuals break down large tasks into smaller, more manageable parts. This makes the task seem less daunting and easier to complete.

e. **Eliminating distractions:** Distractions can significantly reduce productivity. Productive individuals eliminate or minimize distractions, such as social media notifications, emails, or phone calls, while working on important tasks.

f. **Learning to say no**: Productive individuals learn to say no to distractions or tasks that do not align with their goals or priorities. This helps them to stay focused on what is important and avoid wasting time on non-essential tasks.

g. **Regular breaks:** Taking regular breaks is another important productivity habit. This helps individuals to recharge their energy and stay focused on their tasks.

By adopting these and other productivity habits, individuals can significantly improve their productivity and achieve their goals more efficiently. It takes time and effort to develop these habits, but the benefits are well worth the investment.

Relationship Habits

Relationship habits are the patterns of behavior that we adopt in our interactions with others. These habits can be positive or negative and can have a significant impact on the quality of our relationships.

Positive relationship habits involve behaviors such as active listening, expressing gratitude, showing empathy, and engaging in open and honest communication. These habits can help to build trust, foster connection, and promote intimacy in our relationships.

Negative relationship habits, on the other hand, can lead to conflict, mistrust, and disconnection. These may include behaviors such as criticism, defensiveness, stonewalling, and contempt. When we engage in these negative habits, we create barriers to effective communication and may erode the foundation of our relationships over time.

Developing positive relationship habits requires a willingness to be vulnerable and open to feedback. We can start by identifying areas where we may be engaging in negative habits and working to replace them with positive ones. This may involve practicing active listening, expressing appreciation and gratitude, and approaching difficult conversations with an attitude of curiosity and openness.

By developing positive relationship habits, we can build stronger, more fulfilling connections with others and enhance our overall well-being.

Financial Habits

Financial habits refer to the regular and consistent behaviors that individuals engage in when it comes to managing their money. These habits can significantly impact a person's financial well-being and stability.

Developing positive financial habits can help individuals avoid financial stress and achieve their financial goals. Here are some essential financial habits:

a. **Budgeting:** Creating and sticking to a budget is one of the most important financial habits. A budget helps individuals track their spending, plan for expenses, and avoid overspending.

b. **Saving:** Saving regularly, even if it's a small amount, can help individuals build an emergency fund and work towards long-term financial goals like retirement.

c. **Investing:** Investing can help individuals grow their wealth over time. However, it's important to research and understand the risks and potential rewards before investing.

d. **Managing debt:** Managing debt responsibly, such as paying bills on time, paying off high-interest debt first, and avoiding unnecessary debt, can help individuals maintain good credit and avoid financial troubles.

e. **Smart spending:** Being mindful of spending habits can help individuals avoid impulse purchases and unnecessary expenses.

Developing positive financial habits requires discipline and consistency, but the rewards can be significant. By managing money effectively, individuals can reduce financial stress and achieve financial stability and security.

Personal Development Habits

Personal development habits refer to intentional and consistent actions taken to improve oneself and one's life. These habits focus on self-awareness, self-improvement, and growth in various aspects of life, including emotional, intellectual, and spiritual development.

Here are some examples of personal development habits:

a. **Meditation and mindfulness:** Practicing meditation and mindfulness can help individuals develop self-awareness and reduce stress.

b. **Reading:** Consistently reading books can help individuals expand their knowledge and understanding of various subjects and improve their cognitive abilities.

c. **Journaling:** Writing in a journal can help individuals reflect on their thoughts and emotions, gain clarity, and track progress toward their personal goals.

d. **Exercise:** Engaging in regular physical exercise can improve physical health, reduce stress and anxiety, and increase self-confidence.

e. **Learning new skills:** Learning new skills, whether through formal education or informal means, can help individuals develop new talents and abilities, expand their knowledge, and increase their employability.

f.   **Networking:** Building and maintaining a network of professional and personal contacts can provide individuals with support, opportunities for growth, and new perspectives.

Developing personal development habits can improve one's overall well-being and quality of life. These habits can lead to increased self-awareness, personal growth, and a greater sense of fulfillment and purpose.

The Science of Habit Change

- **The 21-day Myth**

The 21-day myth is a commonly held belief that it takes 21 days to form a habit. This idea originated from the work of plastic surgeon Dr. Maxwell Maltz, who observed that it took his patients around 21 days to get used to their new appearance after surgery. However, Maltz did not conduct any scientific research to support his claim.

In reality, the time it takes to form a habit varies greatly depending on the person, the behavior being changed, and the circumstances surrounding the behavior. According to a study published in the European Journal of Social Psychology, it can take anywhere from 18 to 254 days for a habit to become automatic, with an average of around 66 days. The study found that habit formation was more difficult for complex behaviors and behaviors that required significant effort or motivation.

It's important to note that simply repeating a behavior for a certain number of days does not guarantee that it will become a habit. The habit loop (cue, routine, reward) must also be present and reinforced for the behavior to become automatic.

It's also worth mentioning that the idea of the 21-day myth can be harmful in that it creates unrealistic expectations and can lead to frustration and self-doubt when a habit is not formed within this timeframe. Rather than focusing on a specific number of days, it's more important to approach habit formation with patience, consistency, and a willingness to adapt and overcome obstacles.

▪ The Power of Small Wins

The power of small wins is a concept that suggests that achieving small goals or victories can have a positive impact on our overall well-being and motivation. This concept was first introduced by social psychologist Karl Weick in the 1980s and has since been applied to various fields, including personal development, health, and productivity.

The idea behind the power of small wins is that by setting achievable goals and celebrating small successes, we can create a sense of momentum and motivation that can propel us forward toward larger goals. This approach focuses on progress rather than perfection and encourages individuals to break down larger goals into smaller, more manageable steps.

Research has shown that the power of small wins can have a significant impact on our behavior and motivation. For example, a study conducted by Teresa Amabile and Steven Kramer found that individuals who experienced small wins throughout the day reported feeling more motivated and engaged at work. Similarly, a study conducted by social psychologist Roy Baumeister found that individuals who set and achieved small goals throughout the day were more likely to maintain self-control and resist temptation.

The power of small wins can be applied to developing positive habits in a number of ways. For example, instead of trying to overhaul your entire routine overnight, focus on making small changes and celebrating each accomplishment. This could involve setting a goal to meditate for just five minutes a day or to take a 10-minute walk during your lunch break. By achieving these small wins, you may find that you feel more motivated and empowered to tackle larger goals.

The power of small wins emphasizes the importance of celebrating small successes and making progress toward larger goals. By focusing on achievable goals and celebrating each accomplishment, we can create a sense of momentum and motivation that can help us develop positive habits and achieve our goals.

▪ The Importance of Consistency

The importance of consistency in developing positive habits cannot be overstated. Consistency refers to the ability to stick to a routine or behavior over time, regardless of external circumstances or fluctuations in motivation. It is the key ingredient that turns sporadic efforts into lasting change.

Consistency is crucial for several reasons. Firstly, it builds momentum. When we engage in a behavior consistently, it becomes easier to maintain and becomes ingrained in our daily lives. It becomes a natural part of our routine, making it more likely to continue in the long run.

Secondly, consistency reinforces neural pathways in the brain. Our brains are wired to seek efficiency and create automatic responses to repeated behaviors. By consistently engaging in a positive habit, we strengthen these neural pathways, making the behavior more automatic and reducing the effort required to sustain it.

Consistency also helps to overcome resistance and obstacles. When we commit to a habit and remain consistent, we are better equipped to overcome challenges and setbacks that may arise along the way. By maintaining consistency, we build resilience and determination, enabling us to persevere through difficulties.

Moreover, consistency brings about cumulative progress. Small actions performed consistently over time lead to significant results. It is the accumulation of these small efforts that creates substantial changes and positive outcomes. Each day of consistency contributes to overall growth and improvement.

Consistency is also closely tied to self-discipline and willpower. By committing to a habit and following through consistently, we strengthen our self-control and ability to resist temptations or distractions that may hinder our progress. It helps to reinforce our sense of commitment and personal integrity.

To cultivate consistency, it is essential to set realistic and achievable goals. Start with small, manageable steps that you can easily integrate into your daily routine. Focus on building a solid foundation before expanding your efforts. Create a schedule or a system that supports your habit and eliminates unnecessary barriers or distractions. Hold yourself accountable and track your progress to stay motivated.

Incorporating mindfulness and meditation practices can also enhance consistency. These practices cultivate present-moment awareness, help manage distractions, and strengthen focus and determination.

Consistency is a vital component in developing positive habits. It builds momentum, strengthens neural pathways, overcomes obstacles, and leads to cumulative progress. By embracing consistency, we harness the power to create lasting change and achieve optimal health and productivity.

- **The Role of Willpower**

Willpower refers to the ability to control impulses and exert self-control in the pursuit of long-term goals. It is a crucial component in developing positive habits, as it helps individuals resist the temptation to engage in harmful or counterproductive behaviours and instead maintain consistent efforts toward achieving their desired outcomes.

Studies have shown that willpower is a finite resource that can be depleted over time. This means that individuals who rely solely on willpower to develop positive habits may experience difficulty sustaining their efforts in the long run. For this reason, it is important to develop strategies that support the cultivation of willpower, such as establishing a supportive environment, minimizing distractions, and practicing self-care.

One effective way to conserve willpower is to create an environment that promotes positive habits. This may involve removing distractions, such as social media or other time-consuming activities, and surrounding oneself with people who support and encourage the development of healthy habits. By creating a supportive environment, individuals can reduce the amount of willpower needed to maintain their efforts, making it easier to sustain positive habits over time.

Another important aspect of developing positive habits is practicing self-care. This involves taking care of one's physical, mental, and emotional well-being, which can help to reduce stress and improve overall resilience. Simple practices such as getting enough sleep, eating well, and engaging in regular exercise can all contribute to a greater sense of well-being, making it easier to maintain positive habits.

In addition, it is important to acknowledge that setbacks and failures are a normal part of the habit development process. Rather than allowing these setbacks to undermine one's efforts, it is important to practice self-compassion and resilience and to view setbacks as opportunities for learning and growth.

Ultimately, while willpower plays an important role in habit development, it is important to recognize that it is a limited resource that needs to be replenished and supported over time. By creating a supportive environment, practicing self-care, and viewing setbacks as opportunities for growth, individuals can cultivate the resilience and consistency needed to maintain positive habits and achieve long-term success.

▪ The Impact of the Environment on Habits

The environment we live in has a significant impact on our habits. Our daily routines and habits are greatly influenced by the physical and social environment around us. Our environment can either support or sabotage our efforts to develop positive habits.

For example, if we want to develop a habit of exercising every morning, we need to create an environment that supports this habit. This might involve setting out our workout clothes the night before, having a designated workout space, and removing any barriers to exercise, such as scheduling conflicts or lack of equipment. By creating an environment that supports our habit, we increase the likelihood of sticking to it.

On the other hand, if we want to break a bad habit such as smoking, we need to identify and avoid environmental triggers that reinforce this habit. This might involve avoiding social situations where smoking is common or removing smoking paraphernalia from our surroundings.

In addition to the physical environment, our social environment also plays a crucial role in shaping our habits. Our friends, family, and coworkers can either support or undermine our efforts to develop positive habits. If we surround ourselves with people who engage in healthy habits, we are more likely to adopt those habits ourselves. Conversely, if we spend time with people who engage in unhealthy habits, we are more likely to adopt those habits as well.

To create an environment that supports positive habits, we can take proactive steps such as surrounding ourselves with supportive people, setting up our physical environment to support our habits, and avoiding environmental triggers that reinforce bad habits. By doing so, we increase the likelihood of developing and maintaining positive habits over the long term.

Techniques For Developing Positive Habits

- **Mindfulness and Meditation**

Mindfulness and meditation can be powerful tools for developing positive habits. Both practices involve paying attention to the present moment and developing a non-judgmental awareness of one's thoughts, feelings, and bodily sensations.

Mindfulness can help individuals become more aware of their habits and the triggers that lead to them. By cultivating a greater sense of awareness, individuals may be better able to recognize the habits they want to change and make conscious choices about their behavior.

Meditation can also support the development of positive habits by strengthening the prefrontal cortex, the area of the brain responsible for decision-making, impulse control, and planning. A stronger prefrontal cortex can lead to better self-regulation, making it easier to resist temptation and make positive choices.

In addition, meditation and mindfulness practices can help individuals manage stress, anxiety, and other negative emotions that can interfere with the development of positive habits. By cultivating a greater sense of inner peace and emotional stability, individuals may be better equipped to overcome obstacles and maintain their commitment to positive change.

Overall, mindfulness and meditation can be valuable tools for individuals seeking to develop positive habits, as they can help cultivate greater awareness, self-regulation, and emotional well-being.

- **Goal Setting and Planning**

Goal setting and planning are essential components of developing positive habits. Without clear goals and a plan to achieve them, it can be difficult to establish and maintain new habits. Setting goals helps to provide a sense of direction and purpose and helps to motivate and inspire individuals to take action towards achieving their desired outcomes.

When setting goals, it is important to make them specific, measurable, achievable, relevant, and time-bound (SMART). This means that goals should be clearly defined, measurable, realistic, and have a deadline for completion. For example, instead of setting a vague goal like "exercise more," a SMART goal would be "exercise for 30 minutes three times a week for the next three months."

Once goals have been established, creating a plan for achieving them is important. This may involve breaking down the goal into smaller, more manageable steps and identifying potential obstacles and solutions to overcome them. It can also be helpful to establish accountability and support, such as finding a workout partner or hiring a coach, to help you stay on track and motivated.

In addition to setting and planning for specific goals, it can also be helpful to establish daily habits that support overall health and well-being. This may include incorporating mindfulness and meditation practices into daily routines, taking regular breaks to move and stretch throughout the day, and prioritizing self-care activities like getting adequate sleep and eating a balanced diet.

Overall, goal setting and planning are important tools for developing positive habits that support optimal health and productivity. By taking intentional and consistent action towards specific goals and establishing supportive daily habits, individuals can create lasting change and achieve their desired outcomes.

- **Tracking Progress and Accountability**

Tracking progress and accountability are crucial elements of developing positive habits. Tracking your progress helps you to stay motivated and engaged in the habit-building process, while accountability ensures that you stick to your commitments and stay on track toward your goals.

Tracking your progress can take many forms, depending on the habit you are trying to build. For example, if your goal is to exercise more frequently, you might track the number of workouts you complete each week or the amount of time you spend exercising each day. If you are trying to eat healthier, you might track the number of servings of fruits and vegetables you consume each day or the number of calories you consume.

One effective way to track your progress is to use a habit tracker, which is a tool that helps you keep track of your habits and monitor your progress over time. Habit trackers can be physical or digital and can range from simple checklists to complex apps. The key is to find a method that works for you and that you are likely to stick with over the long term.

In addition to tracking your progress, accountability is also important for habit development. Accountability involves making a commitment to someone else to stick to your habit and then following through on that commitment.

This can take many forms, including:

a. Working with a coach or mentor who can help you stay on track and provide guidance and support.

b. Joining a support group or community of people who share your goals can provide encouragement and accountability.

c. Sharing your progress with a friend or family member who can hold you accountable and offer support and encouragement.

The important thing is to find a system of accountability that works for you and that you are willing to commit to. By tracking your progress and holding yourself accountable, you will be much more likely to stick to your habits and achieve your goals.

- **Creating A Supportive Environment**

Creating a supportive environment is crucial when it comes to developing and maintaining positive habits. Your environment can greatly impact your behavior, and if you want to make a change, you need to set yourself up for success by creating an environment that supports your goals.

Here are some tips for creating a supportive environment:

a. **Clear out the clutter:** A cluttered environment can lead to a cluttered mind. Start by decluttering your physical space and creating a clean and organized environment that allows you to focus on your goals.

b. **Surround yourself with positive influences:** Surround yourself with people who support and encourage your goals. Avoid those who may discourage or distract you from your efforts.

c. **Use visual reminders:** Place visual reminders of your goals in areas where you spend the most time. This can be in the form of post-it notes, a vision board, or even a screensaver on your phone or computer.

d. **Make healthy options easily accessible:** Keep healthy snacks, water, and exercise equipment easily accessible to help you make healthier choices throughout the day.

e. **Set boundaries:** Identify the things that may be hindering your progress, such as social media or television, and set boundaries around them. Limit your time spent on these activities and replace them with activities that align with your goals.

f. **Celebrate your progress:** Celebrate your successes, no matter how small they may seem. Rewarding yourself for reaching milestones can help motivate you to continue on your path.

By creating a supportive environment, you are setting yourself up for success in developing positive habits. Remember, your environment can greatly impact your behavior, so make sure it supports the habits you want to develop.

- **Practicing Self-Compassion and Resilience**

Practicing self-compassion and resilience is an essential part of developing positive habits. When we are trying to create new habits or break old ones, it's common to experience setbacks, failures, and moments of self-doubt. However, self-compassion and resilience can help us stay on track and move forward despite these obstacles.

Self-compassion involves treating yourself with kindness, understanding, and acceptance, even when you fall short of your goals or expectations. Instead of beating yourself up for mistakes or failures, self-compassion involves recognizing that everyone makes mistakes, and that failure is a natural part of the learning process. By practicing self-compassion, you can avoid the negative self-talk that often accompanies setbacks and instead focus on what you can learn from the experience.

Resilience is the ability to bounce back from difficult or challenging situations. When we are trying to develop positive habits, we may face obstacles such as a lack of motivation, temptation, or unexpected events that disrupt our routines. Resilience allows us to adapt to these challenges and continue making progress toward our goals. By developing resilience, we can avoid giving up on our habits when faced with setbacks and instead find ways to overcome the obstacles in our path.

Some strategies for practicing self-compassion and resilience include:

a. **Practice mindfulness and self-awareness.** Pay attention to your thoughts and feelings, and notice when you are being self-critical or experiencing negative emotions. By becoming more aware of your inner dialogue, you can start to challenge negative thoughts and replace them with more compassionate and positive ones.

b. **Cultivate a growth mindset.** Instead of seeing setbacks as evidence of your inadequacy, view them as opportunities for learning and growth. Embrace challenges and focus on the progress you are making rather than getting caught up in perfectionism or all-or-nothing thinking.

c. **Build a supportive network.** Surround yourself with people who encourage and support your efforts to develop positive habits. Seek out friends or mentors who can offer guidance, accountability, and a listening ear when you need it.

d. **Practice self-care.** Take care of your physical, emotional, and mental health by eating well, getting enough sleep, and engaging in activities that bring you joy and relaxation. When you are feeling your best, you will be better equipped to handle challenges and setbacks.

By practicing self-compassion and resilience, you can develop the inner strength and resilience needed to create lasting positive habits. These skills can not only help you achieve your personal goals but can also benefit your relationships, work, and overall well-being.

Overcoming Common Obstacles to Habit Change

- **Lack of Motivation**

Motivation can be described as the driving force behind our actions and behaviors. It is the reason why we do what we do, whether it is to achieve a specific goal or to satisfy a need. However, there are times when we may find ourselves lacking the motivation needed to engage in certain activities or pursue certain goals.

There can be many factors that contribute to a lack of motivation. One of the most common causes is feeling overwhelmed or stressed. When we are dealing with a lot of stress or pressure, it can be difficult to focus on anything else, and we may feel as though we do not have the energy or motivation to do anything else.

Another common cause of a lack of motivation is a lack of clear goals or direction. Without a clear sense of purpose or direction, it can be difficult to stay motivated and engaged in any activity or goal. Additionally, if we feel as though our efforts are not producing the desired results, we may become discouraged and lose motivation.

In order to overcome a lack of motivation, it can be helpful to identify the underlying causes and address them directly. For example, if stress is the primary cause, it may be helpful to practice stress-reducing techniques such as mindfulness or meditation. If a lack of clear goals or direction is the issue, setting specific, achievable goals and creating a plan to achieve them can help provide a sense of purpose and direction.

Another effective way to overcome a lack of motivation is to seek support from others. Whether it is through accountability partners, coaches, or mentors, having someone to hold us accountable and provide encouragement and support can help us stay motivated and on track.

It is also important to practice self-compassion and be patient with ourselves. Developing new habits or pursuing challenging goals can be difficult, and setbacks and failures are a natural part of the process. However, by practicing self-compassion and viewing these setbacks as opportunities to learn and grow, we can stay motivated and resilient in the face of challenges.

▪ Procrastination

Procrastination is a common habit that can hinder our productivity and prevent us from achieving our goals. It is the act of delaying or postponing tasks that need to be completed, often until the last minute, despite knowing that it will cause stress and anxiety in the long run. Procrastination can be caused by a variety of reasons, including lack of motivation, fear of failure, and lack of focus.

One way to overcome procrastination is to understand the underlying reasons behind it. For example, if procrastination is caused by fear of failure, it may be helpful to break down the task into smaller, more manageable steps and focus on the progress made rather than the end result. Additionally, identifying and challenging negative self-talk and limiting beliefs can help to overcome the fear of failure.

Another effective strategy is to set specific goals and deadlines. This creates a sense of urgency and accountability, which can motivate us to take action and complete the task. It is also important to prioritize tasks and focus on the most important and urgent ones first rather than getting bogged down in less important tasks.

Eliminating distractions and creating a conducive environment for work can also help to overcome procrastination. This can include minimizing social media use, turning off notifications, and setting aside dedicated time for work without any interruptions.

Lastly, it is important to practice self-compassion and forgive oneself for past procrastination. We are all human and prone to making mistakes, and it is important to approach ourselves with kindness and understanding rather than self-criticism. By adopting a growth mindset and focusing on progress rather than perfection, we can develop a more positive and productive relationship with work and overcome procrastination.

▪ Overcoming Negative Self-talk

Overcoming negative self-talk is an essential aspect of developing positive habits and improving overall well-being. Negative self-talk refers to the critical and self-defeating thoughts and beliefs we have about ourselves, our abilities, and our worth. It can hinder our progress, erode our self-confidence, and limit our potential. However, with mindful awareness and specific techniques, we can learn to challenge and reframe negative self-talk, cultivating a more positive and empowering mindset.

One effective approach to overcoming negative self-talk is to practice self-awareness. Start by paying attention to your inner dialogue and becoming aware of the negative thoughts that arise. Notice the specific language and tone you use when speaking to yourself. This awareness alone can help you recognize the patterns of negative self-talk and the impact they have on your emotions and actions.

Once you are aware of negative self-talk, it is important to challenge its validity. Ask yourself if the thoughts and beliefs you hold about yourself are based on objective evidence or if they are distorted by biases, past experiences, or unfounded fears. Often, negative self-talk is based on irrational or exaggerated thinking. By questioning the accuracy of these thoughts, you can begin to replace them with more realistic and constructive perspectives.

Another powerful technique is to reframe negative self-talk into positive and affirming statements. Replace self-critical thoughts with self-compassionate and encouraging ones. For example, if you catch yourself thinking, "I always mess things up," reframe it as "I am learning and growing from my experiences." Practice affirmations and repeat positive statements to yourself regularly. By consciously choosing empowering thoughts, you can reshape your self-perception and boost your self-esteem.

Mindfulness and meditation can also be effective tools for overcoming negative self-talk. These practices cultivate present-moment awareness and non-judgmental acceptance of thoughts and emotions. By observing negative thoughts without attaching to them or believing in their validity, you can create distance and reduce their impact on your self-image. Meditation helps to calm the mind and develop a sense of inner peace and clarity, making it easier to identify and challenge negative self-talk.

Additionally, surrounding yourself with a supportive network of friends, mentors, or coaches can provide encouragement and help you gain perspective when facing negative self-talk. Sharing your struggles and seeking guidance from others who have overcome similar challenges can be empowering and affirming.

Remember, overcoming negative self-talk is a process that requires patience and persistence. Be gentle with yourself as you navigate this journey and celebrate small victories along the way. With consistent practice and self-compassion, you can rewire your thinking patterns and develop a more positive and empowering self-talk that supports your growth, success, and well-being.

- **Dealing with Setbacks and Failures**

Developing positive habits is an essential part of achieving optimal health and productivity. However, setbacks and failures are inevitable on the road to habit formation. It is important to learn how to deal with these setbacks and failures in a constructive way to avoid getting discouraged and giving up on your goals.

The first step in dealing with setbacks and failures is to

acknowledge and accept them. Instead of beating yourself up over the setback or failure, take a step back and recognize that it is a natural part of the learning process. Use this opportunity to learn from your mistakes and adjust your approach to habit formation accordingly.

Next, focus on the progress you have made so far. It is easy to get caught up in the setback or failure and forget about all the progress you have made up to that point. Reflect on the positive changes that you have already made in your life and use them as motivation to continue working towards your goals.

Another helpful strategy is to reframe your thinking about setbacks and failures. Instead of seeing them as a reflection of your abilities or worth, view them as opportunities for growth and learning. Approach them with a growth mindset, recognizing that every setback and failure is an opportunity to learn, improve, and become stronger.

In addition, it is important to practice self-compassion and avoid negative self-talk. Be kind to yourself and treat yourself with the same compassion and understanding that you would offer to a friend. Acknowledge that setbacks and failures are a natural part of the learning process and that they do not define you as a person.

Finally, it can be helpful to seek support from others. Share your struggles and setbacks with trusted friends or family members who can offer encouragement, support, and advice. Consider joining a support group or seeking professional help from a therapist or coach who can offer additional guidance and support.

Dealing with setbacks and failures is an important part of the habit formation process. By acknowledging and accepting setbacks, focusing on progress, reframing your thinking, practicing self-compassion, and seeking support, you can overcome obstacles and continue to make progress toward your goals.

- **Maintaining momentum and consistency**

Maintaining momentum and consistency is a crucial factor in the development of positive habits. It can be easy to start strong and make progress in the beginning, but it can be much harder to sustain that progress over time. Consistency is essential for building habits because habits require repetition and consistency to become ingrained in our daily lives. Here are some tips for maintaining momentum and consistency in habit formation:

a. **Set realistic goals:** Setting realistic goals is essential for maintaining momentum and consistency. It can be tempting to set lofty goals, but if they are too difficult to achieve, it can lead to frustration and a lack of motivation. Start with small, achievable goals and build from there.

b. **Create a routine:** Habits are easier to maintain when they are part of a routine. Create a daily or weekly routine that includes time for your habit. Make it a non-negotiable part of your day or week.

c. **Use reminders:** Use reminders to help you stay on track. This can include setting reminders on your phone or placing notes around your home or office to remind you of your habit.

d. **Celebrate progress:** Celebrate your progress along the way. Acknowledge and celebrate each small win, no matter how small it may seem. Celebrating progress can help you stay motivated and build momentum.

e. **Find an accountability partner:** Find someone who can hold you accountable for your habit. This can be a friend, family member, or even a professional coach. Having someone who can provide support and hold you accountable can be a powerful motivator.

f. **Practice self-compassion:** Remember that setbacks and mistakes are a normal part of the habit formation process. Be kind to yourself and practice self-compassion. Use setbacks as an opportunity to learn and grow rather than a reason to give up.

By following these tips, you can maintain momentum and consistency in your habit formation journey. Remember that building positive habits is a process, and it takes time, patience, and persistence to achieve lasting change.

Conclusion

Summary of Key Points

In this chapter on developing positive habits, we've explored various strategies for establishing and maintaining healthy habits. We began by discussing the importance of mindfulness and meditation as foundational practices for developing self-awareness and creating a positive mindset. We then delved into the psychology of habit formation, discussing concepts such as the 21-day myth, the power of small wins, and the role of willpower in establishing new habits.

Next, we explored the various factors that can influence our ability to establish and maintain healthy habits, including the impact of our environment, the importance of goal setting and planning, and the need for accountability and tracking progress. We also discussed the importance of creating a supportive environment and practicing self-compassion and resilience when setbacks and failures occur.

Finally, we addressed common obstacles that can hinder habit formation, such as lack of motivation, procrastination, negative self-talk, and dealing with setbacks and failures. We provided practical tips for overcoming these obstacles and maintaining momentum and consistency.

Overall, the key takeaway from this chapter is that developing positive habits is a process that requires patience, persistence, and self-awareness. By utilizing the strategies and techniques discussed in this chapter, you can create healthy habits that will support your overall health and productivity and help you achieve your personal and professional goals.

Final Thoughts and Encouragement to Start Developing Positive Habits.

Congratulations on reaching the end of this chapter on developing positive habits! By now, you should have a good understanding of what habits are, how they are formed, and how they can be changed to improve your health, productivity, and overall well-being.

Throughout this chapter, we've explored various strategies and techniques for developing positive habits, including goal setting, planning, tracking progress, creating a supportive environment, practicing self-compassion and resilience, and overcoming common obstacles such as lack of motivation and procrastination.

It's important to remember that developing positive habits is a process that takes time and effort. You may experience setbacks and failures along the way, but it's important to stay resilient and continue moving forward. Remember to be kind to yourself and practice self-compassion, as developing new habits can be challenging.

Here are some final thoughts and encouragement to start developing positive habits:

a. **Start small:** Don't try to change all your habits at once. Instead, focus on developing one or two small habits at a time, and build from there.

b. **Be consistent:** Habits are formed through repetition, so it's important to be consistent in your efforts. Set aside time each day to practice your new habit, and make it a priority.

c. **Practice mindfulness and meditation:** Mindfulness and meditation can help you stay focused, reduce stress, and increase self-awareness, which can all be helpful in developing positive habits.

d. **Seek support:** Surround yourself with people who support your efforts to develop positive habits, and don't be afraid to ask for help or accountability.

e. **Celebrate your successes:** Recognize and celebrate your progress, no matter how small. This can help keep you motivated and on track.

Remember, developing positive habits is a lifelong process. With persistence, patience, and the right strategies, you can cultivate habits that will help you achieve your goals and live a happier, healthier life.

Chapter 8

STRENGTHENING THE MIND-BODY CONNECTION

This chapter focuses on strengthening the mind-body connection. The mind and body are closely interconnected, and taking care of one can greatly benefit the other. The chapter explores how mindfulness and meditation practices can help improve the mind-body connection, leading to better overall health and well-being.

The chapter covers several topics, including:

1. **Understanding the mind-body connection**: This section explains what the mind-body connection is, how it works, and why it's important to maintain a strong connection between the two.

2. **Mindfulness practices for improving the mind-body connection**: This section explores how mindfulness practices, such as body scans, mindful breathing, and mindful movement, can help improve the mind-body connection by bringing attention to the physical sensations of the body.

3. **Meditation practices for improving the mind-body connection**: This section explains how meditation practices, such as loving-kindness meditation and body-awareness

meditation, can help improve the mind-body connection by cultivating awareness of the body and its sensations.

4. **Yoga as a practice for strengthening the mind-body connection:** This section explores how yoga, a mind-body practice that combines physical postures with breath control and meditation, can help improve the mind-body connection by increasing body awareness and reducing stress.

5. **The role of nutrition in the mind-body connection:** This section discusses the important role that nutrition plays in maintaining a strong mind-body connection, including the benefits of eating a balanced diet and staying hydrated.

6. **The impact of sleep on the mind-body connection:** This section explores how getting enough sleep is essential for maintaining a strong mind-body connection, including the benefits of a good night's sleep and tips for improving sleep hygiene.

7. **Developing a holistic approach to health and well-being:** This section emphasizes the importance of taking a holistic approach to health and well-being, which includes not only physical health but also mental and emotional health. It encourages readers to cultivate self-care practices that support the mind-body connection and overall well-being.

Overall, this chapter aims to provide readers with a comprehensive understanding of the mind-body connection and practical tools and strategies for strengthening it. By cultivating a strong mind-body connection, readers can improve their physical health, mental and emotional well-being, and overall quality of life.

Understanding the Mind-Body Connection

The mind-body connection is the relationship between our mental and physical states. It's the way our thoughts, emotions, and beliefs influence our physical health and well-being. The mind and body are not separate entities but rather interconnected systems that work together to create our overall health and experience.

When we experience stress, anxiety, or negative emotions, our body responds by releasing hormones like cortisol and adrenaline, which can lead to physical symptoms like headaches, muscle tension, and digestive issues. On the other hand, positive emotions like joy, gratitude, and love can have a healing effect on our body, boosting our immune system and promoting overall well-being.

Research has shown that there are several ways in which the mind-body connection works. For example, the autonomic nervous system (ANS) plays a crucial role in regulating our body's response to stress. When we're stressed, the sympathetic branch of the ANS is activated, leading to the release of stress hormones and a fight-or-flight response. However, when we engage in relaxation techniques like deep breathing or meditation, the parasympathetic branch of the ANS is activated, leading to a state of relaxation and calmness.

Another way in which the mind-body connection works is through the placebo effect. This is the phenomenon where a person experiences a beneficial effect from a treatment that has no active ingredient. The placebo effect is believed to work through the power of suggestion and the person's belief that the treatment will work.

Maintaining a strong mind-body connection is essential for optimal health and well-being. By becoming more aware of our thoughts, emotions, and physical sensations, we can learn to manage stress and improve our overall health. This can be achieved through practices like mindfulness, meditation, yoga, and other relaxation techniques.

In the following sections of this chapter, we will explore various ways to strengthen the mind-body connection and how it can benefit our overall health and productivity. We will also look at how different factors like diet, exercise, and sleep can impact the mind-body connection and provide tips for maintaining a healthy balance between the two.

Mindfulness Practices for Improving the Mind-Body Connection

In this section of Chapter 8, we will delve into the various mindfulness practices that can help strengthen the mind-body connection. Mindfulness is the practice of bringing your full attention to the present moment without judgment. By focusing on the present moment and bringing awareness to your bodily sensations, you can improve your mind-body connection.

One mindfulness practice that can be helpful is a body scan. A body scan involves lying down in a comfortable position and directing your attention to different parts of your body, starting at your toes and moving up to the top of your head. As you focus on each body part, you can bring awareness to any sensations, such as tension, warmth, or tingling. This practice can help you become more in tune with your body and its signals, leading to a stronger mind-body connection.

Mindful breathing is another practice that can improve the mind-body connection. By focusing on your breath and the sensations in your body as you breathe, you can bring yourself into the present moment and become more aware of your body's signals. You can practice mindful breathing by taking deep, intentional breaths and focusing on the rise and fall of your chest and belly.

Mindful movements, such as yoga or Tai Chi, can also be a helpful practice for improving the mind-body connection. By focusing on your breath and the movements of your body as you move, you can become more in tune with your physical sensations and improve your body awareness.

Overall, incorporating mindfulness practices into your daily routine can help you develop a stronger mind-body connection. By paying attention to the physical sensations of your body and bringing awareness to the present moment, you can improve your overall health and well-being.

Meditation Practices for Improving the Mind-Body Connection

Meditation is a powerful tool that can help individuals strengthen their mind-body connection. Through meditation, individuals can cultivate greater awareness of their physical sensations, thoughts, and emotions, which in turn can help them better understand and connect with their bodies.

One meditation practice that can be particularly effective for improving the mind-body connection is loving-kindness meditation. This practice involves sending positive, loving thoughts and feelings to oneself and others, which can help individuals develop a greater sense of compassion and connection with themselves and others.

Body-awareness meditation is another effective practice for improving the mind-body connection. This practice involves bringing awareness to the physical sensations of the body, such as the sensations of the breath, the feelings of tension or relaxation in the muscles, and any other bodily sensations that may arise. By cultivating this awareness, individuals can learn to better understand and connect with their bodies and can develop greater control over their physical and emotional responses.

Other types of meditation, such as mindfulness meditation and guided imagery, can also be effective for improving the mind-body connection. These practices involve bringing attention to the present moment and can help individuals cultivate greater awareness of their physical sensations, thoughts, and emotions. By practicing meditation regularly, individuals can develop a stronger mind-body connection, which can lead to improved physical and mental health, greater self-awareness, and increased well-being.

Yoga as a Practice for Strengthening the Mind-Body Connection

Yoga is a practice that has been around for thousands of years and is known for its ability to strengthen the mind-body connection. Yoga combines physical postures with breath control and meditation to help practitioners achieve greater awareness of their bodies and minds. In this section, we will explore the benefits of yoga as a practice for strengthening the mind-body connection.

One of the primary ways in which yoga improves the mind-body connection is through increased body awareness. Through practicing yoga, individuals become more attuned to the physical sensations of their bodies. They learn to identify areas of tension or discomfort as well as areas of ease and openness. This heightened awareness of the body allows practitioners to better understand how their physical sensations and emotions are interconnected.

Yoga also helps to reduce stress, which can have a profound impact on the mind-body connection. Chronic stress can lead to physical tension in the body, as well as negative thoughts and emotions. Through practicing yoga, individuals learn to release tension in the body and calm the mind, which can lead to reduced stress levels. This reduction in stress can have a positive impact on both physical and mental health.

In addition to physical postures, yoga also incorporates breath control and meditation. These practices can help individuals to develop greater control over their minds and emotions. Breath control, or pranayama, involves consciously regulating the breath in order to calm the mind and reduce anxiety. Meditation involves focusing the mind on a particular object or idea, such as the breath or a mantra. Through these practices, individuals can develop greater self-awareness and cultivate a sense of inner peace.

Overall, yoga is an excellent practice for strengthening the mind-body connection. Through increased body awareness, reduced stress, and practices such as breath control and meditation, individuals can cultivate greater self-awareness and a sense of inner peace.

The Role of Nutrition in the Mind-Body Connection

The mind and body are intricately connected, and the food we eat has a significant impact on both. A balanced diet that includes a variety of whole foods such as fruits, vegetables, whole grains, lean proteins, and healthy fats can help improve brain function, boost energy levels, and support overall physical health.

In particular, certain nutrients have been shown to have a positive impact on the mind-body connection. For example, omega-3 fatty acids found in fatty fish, nuts, and seeds have been linked to improved cognitive function and reduced inflammation, while B vitamins found in leafy greens, whole grains, and lean meats have been shown to improve mood and reduce stress.

Staying hydrated is also essential for maintaining a strong mind-body connection. Dehydration can lead to fatigue, difficulty concentrating, and even mood swings. It is recommended to drink at least eight glasses of water per day and to consume more water when engaging in physical activity or when in hot weather.

In addition to eating a balanced diet and staying hydrated, it is important to be mindful of any food intolerances or sensitivities that may be impacting your body. Certain foods, such as gluten or dairy, may cause inflammation or digestive issues for some individuals, leading to physical and mental discomfort.

Overall, nutrition plays an important role in strengthening the mind-body connection, and it is important to prioritize a balanced diet and stay hydrated to support both physical and mental health.

The Impact of Sleep on the Mind-Body Connection

Getting enough sleep is critical for maintaining a strong mind-body connection. Sleep is when our bodies repair and regenerate, and it is essential for cognitive function, mood regulation, and overall health. Lack of sleep or poor sleep quality can negatively impact the mind-body connection, leading to decreased focus, increased stress, and a host of physical health problems.

The benefits of a good night's sleep are numerous. Getting enough sleep can improve cognitive function, including memory and concentration, and can help regulate mood, reducing symptoms of depression and anxiety. It also supports physical health, promoting healthy weight management, reducing the risk of chronic diseases such as heart disease and diabetes, and boosting the immune system.

Tips for improving sleep hygiene include establishing a regular sleep routine, including going to bed and waking up at the same time each day; creating a sleep-conducive environment, such as keeping the bedroom cool, dark, and quiet; avoiding electronic devices before bed, and engaging in relaxing activities before sleep, such as reading or meditation.

In addition to these lifestyle factors, some mindfulness practices can also help improve sleep quality and promote a strong mind-body connection. For example, body scan meditations can help release tension in the body and promote relaxation, while deep breathing exercises can help calm the mind and prepare for sleep. Incorporating these practices into a bedtime routine can support restful sleep and contribute to a strong mind-body connection.

Developing a Holistic Approach to Health and Well-Being

Developing a holistic approach to health and well-being involves taking care of all aspects of oneself, including physical, mental, and emotional health. It is important to recognize that the mind and body are interconnected and that one affects the other. Therefore, to achieve optimal health and well-being, it is essential to focus on both the mind and body.

One way to develop a holistic approach to health and well-being is by incorporating self-care practices that support the mind-body connection. This can include regular exercises, such as yoga or walking, mindfulness practices like meditation, and maintaining a healthy diet and good sleep hygiene. Additionally, engaging in activities that bring joy and relaxation, such as spending time in nature, reading, or spending time with loved ones, can also support overall well-being.

It is also important to address any emotional or mental health concerns through therapy or counseling, as these issues can have a significant impact on the mind-body connection. By taking a holistic approach to health and well-being, individuals can better understand the interconnectedness of their mind and body and how each one affects the other.

Incorporating self-care practices that support the mind-body connection can help individuals better manage stress, improve sleep, increase energy and focus, and enhance overall health and well-being.

By cultivating a holistic approach to health and well-being, individuals can lead more fulfilling and satisfying lives.

Chapter 9

CONCLUSION: MIND-BODY MASTERY

As we come to the end of this book on Mind-Body Mastery, I hope that you have gained a deeper understanding of the mind-body connection and the powerful impact it can have on your health, productivity, and overall well-being. We have explored various mindfulness and meditation practices, yoga, nutrition, and sleep as essential tools for strengthening the mind-body connection and achieving optimal health.

My goal in writing this book was to empower you with knowledge and tools that will help you live a more mindful, healthy, and fulfilling life.

I truly believe that by cultivating a strong mind-body connection, you can enhance your physical health, boost your mental clarity and emotional resilience, and live a more productive and joyful life.

I understand that developing positive habits and making lifestyle changes can be challenging, but I encourage you to approach it with patience, compassion, and a growth mindset. It is a journey that requires commitment, consistency, and self-care, but the benefits are immeasurable.

I wish you well on your journey toward Mind-Body Mastery and encourage you to continue exploring and incorporating mindfulness and meditation practices, yoga, and other self-care practices into your daily life. Remember, the key is to find what works best for you and make it a sustainable part of your routine.

Thank you for taking the time to read this book, and I hope that it has been a valuable resource for you. May you continue to thrive and flourish in your pursuit of optimal health and well-being.

We love creating beautiful books for you!

Come be a part of our ever-growing community of authors. Grow, write, and publish with us!

Scan here to explore books, authors and more

Connect with us on socials. We'd love to hear from you!

    Inkfeathers Publishing